A Season of Little Sacraments

A Season of Little Sacraments
Christmas Commotion, Advent Grace

Susan H. Swetnam

LITURGICAL PRESS
Collegeville, Minnesota

www.litpress.org

1   2   3   4   5   6   7   8   9

Library of Congress Cataloging-in-Publication Data

Names: Swetnam, Susan H., author.
Title: A season of little sacraments : Christmas commotion, Advent grace / Susan H. Swetnam.
Description: Collegeville, Minnesota : Liturgical Press, 2016.
Identifiers: LCCN 2016008110 (print) | LCCN 2016022776 (ebook) | ISBN 9780814646724 | ISBN 9780814646977
Subjects: LCSH: Advent—Meditations. | Sacraments—Catholic Church.
Classification: LCC BX2170.A4 S94 2016 (print) | LCC BX2170.A4 (ebook) | DDC 242/.332—dc23
LC record available at https://lccn.loc.gov/2016008110

This book is dedicated to
the Sisters at the Monastery of St. Gertrude,
Cottonwood, Idaho,

friends and mentors who demonstrate how to live
every day in joyful hope.

Contents

Introduction

Inviting the Sacramental into an Ordinary, Jam-Packed, Over-Committed Twenty-First-Century Advent

The lament swells every December, as perennial as the jingle of Salvation Army bells. We've lost "the reason for the season" and have "taken Christ out of Christmas," media commentators and evangelical preachers proclaim. The secular trappings of Christmas—shopping, decorating, partying—have come to dominate our culture so conclusively, these critics contend, that few of us even remember the sacred gift we're celebrating. We need to get back to the basics of faith, to focus on church rather than on these distractions.

Several years ago an idealistic young priest in my Idaho parish embraced this theme with purist zeal. He issued a directive on the feast of Christ the King: we should wait until Christmas to engage in Christmas-y activities. Making an Advent wreath to welcome the season was fine, he granted, but all other decorations—Christmas lights, trees, any form of hall-decking—shouldn't happen before Christmas Eve day. Christmas cards should be sent and delivered during Christmas itself (the canonical period beginning with December 25) and *not* during Advent. Shopping and fancy holiday cooking (unavoidable barnacles on the season, he conceded) should be delayed until the week before Christmas at the earliest.

What should we be doing in the meantime? Coming to church for daily mass as well as on Sundays, walking the Stations of the Cross and eating meager meals on Fridays, holding at least twice-daily devotionals in our homes, purifying ourselves by various kinds of sacrifices. In the early church, he explained, Advent was a period of solemn preparation, a time of fasting and prayer. "It's Advent-as-Lent," one of my friends remarked. She was all in favor of a faith-filled season, she said, but in her opinion such austerity secured Christ's place in December at the expense of joyful anticipation.

We're a parish serious about its faith, one with strong attendance at Mass and at adult theology sessions. We welcome many new members every Easter. We maintain a strong roster of lay ministers and engage in an extensive program of social justice. Still, you can probably imagine the kind of compliance rate our priest achieved both for the things we should have done and for the things we should have left undone. Though many of us did embrace at least some of the practices he suggested, ultimately the prospect of foregoing the pleasure of all modern Christmas preparations proved too much of a challenge. I've always suspected that the poor guy didn't get invited to too many homes during the four weeks of Advent that year, given the guilty evidence of non-compliance I witnessed and compiled in my own home.

That idealistic priest and other critics of twenty-first century Advent do have a point, of course, as anybody who has ever turned on a television on Black Friday must agree. Unseemly shopping frenzies embody the antithesis of "peace on earth"; enticements to spend more every year on gifts not only distract us but lead many into dangerous debt. Season-themed television shows, popular songs, and decorations often ignore the real Christmas. Attempting to replicate the material trappings of a perfect holiday as featured in magazines, we tax our resources and energy. We become irritated, anxious, and uncharitable as the season progresses. Hoping to create the idyllic tableaus of family and personal happiness the media suggests are "normal," we feel frustration with loved ones, depression, self-doubt, and envy when reality does not measure up.

A host of Advent devotional books have appeared in past decades from theologians, priests, monastics, popular religious writers, and editors who compile the words of saints or church fathers. These volumes seek to remind us that there's another Advent behind the commercial Christmas frenzy. Drawing on liturgical scriptural readings and/or specific religious observances within Advent's calendar, like the Feast of St. Lucy or the presentation of Mary in the temple, such works emphasize that Advent should be a season of reverent (and also joyful) waiting, hope, and contemplation of the mystery of Christ's incarnation. Each day readers are invited to join the writers in prayerfully considering the implications of the particular week's texts. These writers put scriptural words into historical, biblical, theological, sociological, and comparative religion contexts; some offer workbook-style questions to inspire the reader's meditation and prayer.

This book also aims to help readers stay awake spiritually in this great season of preparation, but it takes an alternate (some might even think radical) approach to Advent faith formation. Though the chapters that follow certainly allude to the season's ageless and enduring liturgical texts, they stake their ground where most twenty-first-century laypeople *actually live* during Advent, like it or not: in the heart of December's commotion. Those who are fortunate enough to be able to go on retreat or who belong to particular religious orders might be able to escape the month's onslaught of secular Christmas pressure, but the vast majority of us are fooling ourselves if we think we can. Even if we adopt a purist approach to Advent we must, at the very least, go out to work and/or to shop for groceries or other necessities, encountering along the way a culture possessed by holiday craziness.

As this book seeks to demonstrate, however, contemplative isolation is not the only way to live a spiritually-rich Advent. Indeed, my own experience suggests that if we can keep our eyes open and cultivate a reflective habit of mind, the events of ordinary daily life may become rich catalysts for devotional meditation. Even the material rituals of preparing for Christmas—the very "distractions" that are accused of removing Christ from the celebration—can constitute gateways to deeper faith. They can invite us into the heart and soul of Advent's core themes: waiting in patience and hope; acknowledging our own vulnerability, brokenness, and need; reaching to others in a spirit of common humanity; and cultivating joy in the promise of Christ's coming and the assurance of God's essential love.

The idea that the mundane and the sacred can interpenetrate is hardly a new concept in our faith, especially regarding this time of year. Advent, after all, is in its essence about contemplating the mystery of the incarnation. Christ assumes human flesh and enters our sphere, the very domain that includes all the messy joy of December's preparations. This is the same earthly context that once included men who fished from small boats and got their feet dusty as they walked rough roads, a world where women could become so preoccupied with housework that they didn't pay enough attention to an honored guest. People once encountered Jesus in mundane earthly settings, and his grace can still extend into the ordinary secular rush of our lives if we open our ears, our eyes, our hearts to him in the midst of such daily business.

The intersection of the sacred and secular has been a popular theme in religious art across the centuries. The juxtaposition is patently unavoidable in depictions of the annunciation, that central Advent story in which the angel Gabriel appears to the Virgin Mary and announces that she is to bear God's son. This subject was especially popular in the Italian Renaissance, a period when exclusively sacred topics of composition began to give way to secular themes. In their depictions of the annunciation, the era's artists might be said to have split the difference. The subject is canonical; the angel is marvelously supernatural. Yet the Virgin appears not just as an earthly woman but in everyday period settings. The Mary of Italian Renaissance painting walks on a logia porch, sits in a parlor among ordinary domestic trappings, or is interrupted while she reads or does handiwork. The corollary today might be Mary unloading the dishwasher or texting.

Among my favorites in the Mary-interrupted line are the paintings of Florentine artist Alessandro Allori, which show Mary receiving the news while knitting or making lace. Startled by Gabriel, the Virgin has dropped her work onto the floor. All knitters (like me) will be able to identify with an evocative implication of that minor circumstance: once the angel goes back to wherever it is that angels live and the woman in the picture retrieves the piece, she'll certainly have lost her place in the pattern and will most likely discover that she's dropped stitches. As she struggles to take in the monumental new start announced by the angel, she'll discover that she has to begin again in small aspects of her life, too.

We may not be ready for the angel who informs us that God has a plan that will revolutionize our lives. The revelation may come at an inconvenient time. But the ordinary, daily round of life is our sphere, and so that is where the call will come. The mystery and the mundane are inextricably intertwined.

~☙ ~☙ ~☙

The seven great sacraments provide formal and communal opportunities for Catholics to encounter that mystery and receive God's grace. The *Catechism of the Catholic Church* explains that "the visible rites" of baptism, confirmation, the Eucharist, holy orders, matrimony, reconciliation, and the anointing of the sick "signify and make present the graces proper to each" (1131). They "give birth and increase, healing and mission to the Christian's life of faith" (1210). To participate in them is to gain special access to Christ.

Modern theologians have suggested that the receipt of grace is not reserved exclusively for moments in church, however. Encountering Christ "is also at the heart of the specifically human and secular activities that predominate in our lives," writes Jesuit Michael J. Taylor in his introduction to *The Sacraments: Readings in Contemporary Sacramental Theology*. "Grace 'happens' when human life is lived and celebrated authentically."

Working from that premise, this book considers the ordinary "distractions" of contemporary December as potential "little sacraments": opportunities to touch the divine and move closer into alignment with our authentic nature as God's children. Its chapters invite readers along on a very ordinary walk through December, encouraging them by narrative example and reflection to imagine their own seasonal "distractions" as opportunities for the particular sacred graces of Advent to break into their lives. Each chapter is sparked by a twenty-first century component of Christmas preparation and considers an important liturgical theme for the season. These juxtapositions mirror what I (the ordinary woman in question, a Catholic middle-class teacher, writer, and widow living a few miles from a university town in southeastern Idaho) have discovered over many years of seeking to experience Advent with reverent open eyes: that the secular occurrences of our lives, no less than the "churchy" ones, can bring us closer to God.

Most of the chapters that follow are grounded in seasonal activities with which readers will be familiar, including decorating, choosing gifts, braving the stores and traffic, sending Christmas cards, making impossibly ambitious to-do lists, and hosting gatherings large and small. But there are also few chapters that chronicle distinctive, even idiosyncratic, customs of my own. My aim in the range of choices is not to present a universal template for a specific December regimen or to instruct readers in thinking exactly as I do about the particulars of a twenty-first century Advent. Instead I hope that this book will strike at least a few "I've been there"-style chords, suggest new practices readers might want to try, and most of all invite readers to reflect prayerfully for themselves about the sacred implications of their own round of Christmas preparations.

Throughout I intend to demonstrate that it is not as difficult as it might seem to approach real-world seasonal activities with attention to their spiritual ramifications. One only has to pay attention to Advent's call, for God will work with us if we go even a small way out to meet him. We require not perfection in observance but persistence in recalling ourselves to a listening habit of mind after the inevitable slips of attention. It is not too taxing to take just a few times a week to read the season's liturgy and perhaps other texts like this one. Through the practice of prayer or journaling one may build the habit of reflecting consciously on what has happened in the round of daily life. Even baby steps toward staying awake may provide opportunities to live the season reverently, as it is meant to be lived.

Ideally, of course, we might live that way every day, walking mindfully through a world crackling with potential insight. Perhaps some people do—people for whom living and meditating on God's wisdom have become one, for whom reflecting is as natural as breathing not just in Advent, but in all life's seasons.

That's not me, though, and I'm guessing it's not going to be most readers either. Still, one has to begin somewhere. And where better than at the start of the church year, a period when we're explicitly invited to prepare the way of the Lord?

Walk with me through the ordinary, jam-packed, over-committed, distracting, and *sacred* days of a twenty-first century Advent.

Week 1

Opening to a Season
of Longing and Hope

1

Committing to Attention

Making an Advent Playlist

"You listen to Christmas music even when you run?" a friend asked recently as we discussed our respective workout plans for the coming winter. "That's seriously high tolerance. I always get sick of Christmas music weeks before Christmas arrives—it's on the radio, playing in the grocery stores. You can't check the weather on television without hearing it. It was even playing at the dentist's office when I got my teeth cleaned last week. I'm about done already with 'Silent Night' and 'Joy to the World' and 'Sleigh Ride' for this year."

Not Christmas music, I explained. What I'd said was that I always make a playlist of *Advent* music for my December runs.

"Advent music?" She looked puzzled. "What's Advent?"

Advent is such a fixture of the calendar in liturgical Christian churches that it can be surprising to realize that the season is not observed by all sects that consider themselves Christian (my friend's faith tradition is among the latter). Arriving at the start of the church year in late November or the first Sunday of

December, Advent constitutes its own sacred season, a four-week interval distinct from Christmas. It's a time of anticipation and preparation for the coming of Christ. It's a quiet season compared to the great festival that follows, a period when believers are instructed to wait in confident hope, cultivating attention, repentance, charity, and joy.

In the Catholic Church Advent entails its own distinctive rituals. We light an additional candle each Sunday on a wreath of four, for example; we eschew the "Gloria" until Christmas. It brings its own special liturgical readings and violet vestment colors (with rose introduced on the third Sunday—Gaudete Sunday—to signify the joyful anticipation voiced in the Scripture readings). Dearest to my heart among the customs that set Advent apart, however, is its music.

Life would be so much poorer without the songs of Advent— those at-once yearning and joyful strains that mark late November, early and mid-December. Only at this time of year do we hear the cluster of hymns at the very front of the music section of the missal, songs that blend solemn minor keys with encouraging, even confidently peaceful texts. To sing them is to enter into community with many generations of the faithful, many cultures. "Come, Thou Long-Expected Jesus" and "On Jordan's Bank" offer an echo of the eighteenth century. "The King Shall Come When Morning Dawns" reprises an early nineteenth-century Kentucky tune. "See How the Virgin Waits for Him" is set to a traditional Slovakian folk melody and "The Angel Gabriel" to a Basque one. Even the more recently composed Advent hymns sound exotic with their archaic language and rich musical settings: "Come Watch and Wait" and "Beyond the Moon and Stars," for instance.

I, for one, get lonesome for these songs in other seasons. Sometimes in the late summer or early fall, when Ordinary Time can seem extremely ordinary, I feel nostalgia for the drama of their proper season and sneak a peek at them in the missal when I should be concentrating on something else. I'm never "done with them" when we transition to the hymns of Christmas on the night of December 24.

So great is my hunger for these songs that I've been making an Advent playlist for my iPod for the past decade. Yes, I confess: though I'm a woman of a certain age, I've become one of those annoying people who go around the world with little plugs in their ears, listening to music that no one else can hear. Once upon a time I railed at such people, complaining that they had cut themselves off from reality, pitying them for losing the chance to really be here, now. Lately, though, I've come to believe that sometimes it's good to step back—even while engaged in the actual practice of walking (or running) around the planet earth—from the "here" of external details into the internal focus that music can provide.

I listen to my playlist just about every day during Advent, during daily runs that become mini-retreats. Most often those workouts take place in the early morning or at dusk in the national forest a mile beyond my southeastern Idaho home, on a quiet two-lane road that stretches through a canyon beside a dancing creek. When the press of obligations at the regional university where I teach English necessitates lunchtime exercise, I traverse the streets around campus.

Every year's playlist is new, built on Christ-the-King weekend. The process is vastly enjoyable, a happy here-we-go-over-the-falls-into-Advent personal ritual. There's a lot of prospecting on Pandora and in the iTunes store, much importing of songs from seasonal CDs purchased the previous year, a reunion with and rediscovery of old favorites. The sequence gets tinkered with until it's just right. When in doubt, a song always makes the cut.

The selection is shaped by the flavor that life has assumed in that particular year. Instrumentals have dominated lately since they provide more space for meditation, and for the past few Advents responsibilities have filled my days with distracting noise. In the past when life was quieter songs with words appeared in greater proportion.

The list for this year—the year in which I'm compiling these reflections and writing this book—represents a mixture. It's heavy on peaceful piano versions of traditional Advent hymns played by Jeff Bjorck, Vicky Emerson, and others, but it also includes noncanonical Advent-style music, meditative winter compositions by David Lanz and various Wyndham Hill artists. There are varied voices on the playlist, too. A few years ago a Benedictine nun introduced me to Richard Souther's "Vision," a setting of Hildegard of Bingen's music that manages to sound simultaneously postmodern and medieval, and selections from that CD have since appeared annually. Bits of the earliest solos and choruses from Handel's *Messiah* punctuate the instrumentals (not the "Halleluiah Chorus," though—I'm a purist, and that's Easter music!). Choral versions of regular Advent hymns that we sing in church appear on the list, as do Alison Krauss's version of "In the Bleak Midwinter" and some appropriate bluegrass songs.

⌇ ⌇ ⌇

Despite the yearly variations, two selections have been consistent from the list's birth. I imagine that everyone who loves music has songs like this, melodies and words that have become anthems,

cadences that take a person back to times of joy or sorrow. In
the case my Advent playlist, one is contemporary vocalist Amy
Grant's "Breath of Heaven [Mary's Song]," a Christian radio hit
that helped save my life during the third Advent after my husband
Ford died of cancer. Taking big theological chances, its words imagine what Mary might have been thinking during her pregnancy.
The Mary of the song is exhausted and struggling with feelings of
unworthiness; she fears that God may be having second thoughts
about choosing her. Nevertheless, true to the biblical words of
the *Magnificat* she offers herself humbly, acknowledging God's
ultimate wisdom though she cannot understand why he has done
what he has. With simple faith she vows to trust and to carry on.

Back in December of 2004 the initial shock of my husband's
death had long since worn off and I entered Advent exhausted,
angry, depressed, and beginning to fear that such feelings would
never abate. The radio's unrelentingly cheerful pop Christmas
songs depicted a holiday in which everybody seemed to be rev-
eling together and kissing in the snow. That year even the carols
in church hurt, for they invited comparison to past holidays.
I'm afraid that I focused on the references to "toiling along the
climbing way" and "suffering, sighing, bleeding, dying" instead of
the ultimate promises behind those travails.

I felt as though I were looking into the bright windows of
normal life from raw winter darkness outside, a spare part, a
woman now of no consequence to anyone. I lived alone, a fifty-
year-old childless widow, a continent's distance from my mother
and siblings (though richly blessed with friends). Graduate study
had led me from a childhood home in the Philadelphia suburbs
first to Newark, Delaware, and then to Ann Arbor, Michigan. A
tenure-track job had brought me to southeastern Idaho. Though

I'd never been west of Kalamazoo when I arrived for the interview, I knew as soon as the plane banked for landing and the mountain ranges framing the city came into view that Pocatello would be home. After Ford and I met and married, I assumed that we'd live together in this landscape that spoke with such clarity to both of our spirits for many, many years, until we were both decrepit, though I couldn't imagine what that would be like.

All of my cherished plans for the future had crumbled. Even in the worst early days I never entertained the thought of moving away, certainly not back to the east coast. After living in the West, the place where I grew up seems claustrophobic. But how—and why—was I to live without my husband? The church suggested that what had happened was part of God's plan, but I wanted none of it.

Then I met the Mary in "Breath of Heaven." Though the song had been released a decade earlier, it only came to my ears via the car radio that year, a circumstance which might in itself inspire meditation. This Mary was complicated, human, lonely, and yet blessed. This Mary could entertain doubts, yet she remained faithful to the path assigned her. To do God's will, this version of the story suggests, you don't have to feel confident in your capacity to please him. Neither do you have to *like* the hand that God has dealt you. You just have to trust and do the work that's your portion—to "proclaim the greatness of the Lord" even though you cannot begin to understand his ways. "Breath of Heaven" reached viscerally to me that year, and even though I'm now on much firmer ground its message remains relevant.

◦ ◦ ◦

The other perennial feature of my Advent playlist is that most venerable of Advent hymns, "O Come, O Come, Emmanuel."

Its ninth-century words and fifteenth-century chant-style music evoke an ancient longing for God's presence. "O come, O come," we intone at the beginning of each of the myriad verses, inviting the Savior as we name him through a series of mysterious honorifics, properly called "O Antiphons." We are, we admit, a captive and exiled people desperate for ransoming, mere humans who need God to "order[ ] all things mightily," to "close the path to misery," and to help us triumph over death.

As we voice the words of this hymn, we briefly construct ourselves as pre-incarnation people, people for whom this whole salvation thing is still provisional—even though our faith and theology ensure that we know better. We become humble creatures yearning for God to redeem us. This is not a song for people who have been "born again," people certain of their virtue, their worthiness in God's eyes. It's a song for those of us who know that we need grace.

⌦ ⌦ ⌦

Such reflections on acquiescence and trust might seem more appropriately pursued in a cloister or during a structured Advent retreat than while engaged in running around the world dressed in high-tech, twenty-first-century sports fabrics, watching out for cars and curbs and wildlife, checking time and pace on a fancy Garmin watch. It's a weird form of multitasking, I admit, one that might be considered a bit sacrilegious. Shouldn't a person make pristine time utterly apart in this season?

Well, yes, and those of us who actively practice our religion inevitably spend at least some such time in the normal course of Advent observance. We attend Sunday masses, adore the Blessed Sacrament, and participate in reconciliation. We might read devotionals instead of the newspaper with breakfast. Setting apart *substantial every-day time* for personal reflection, though, can prove to be a very difficult commitment. I know that I struggle to honor such an intention in practice, even though I'm a childless widow whose responsibilities include only work, housekeeping, and cultivating friendships, not also caring for a spouse and children.

I've discovered, though, that when such devotion is combined with an ingrained habit it is more likely to become part of a daily routine. I find that making my workout sessions into meditation periods dedicates at least one hour six days a week to absorption in holy concerns. Thus the Advent playlist and the commitment to simultaneous care of body and soul. It's better to invite a daily hour of reflection in that imperfect way, I've come to believe, than to forego the opportunity because it's not pristine.

෴ ෴ ෴

According to the foundational twentieth-century papal letter on sacred music, *Tra le sollecitudini*, issued by Pope Pius X in 1903, the genre should "rouse[ ] the faithful to devotion, and better [dispose them] to gather to themselves the fruits of grace which come from the celebration of the sacred mysteries." As a conservative reformer seeking to purify the Roman Rite from popular or merely theatrical music, Pius might well look askance at some of the individual selections that form my daily Advent soundtrack. He might also disapprove of the circumstances (divorced from liturgical worship) of the delivery. Still, I hope that he'd be sympathetic to the intent.

Many pastoral documents affirming the efficacy of music in faith formation have followed *Tra le sollecitudini*. One of the most important was *Liturgical Music Today*, published in 1972 by the members of the Bishops' Committee on the Liturgy of the National Conference of Catholic Bishops (USA). This statement affords sacred music a privileged place in worship, noting that it "does not serve as a mere accompaniment, but as the integral mode in which the mystery is proclaimed and presented."

⋄ ⋄ ⋄

Out there on the chilly Idaho roads in December the mystery is proclaimed continuously through those earbuds; the devotion is roused as naturally as breathing.

An *Advent* playlist? How can any even marginally tech-saavy Christian live without one?

2

Choosing to Slow Down

Hosting a Wreath-Making Party

"Let every heart prepare him room," asserts the first verse of "Joy to the World"—a 1719 carol so beloved that it has become the most-published Christmas hymn in America. While on a basic level the line alludes to Mary and Joseph's inability to find room at the inn, it also functions as a metaphor. When we prepare Christ room, we open our hearts and lives to what is holy. We drop our defenses and temper our preoccupations so that God's love may enter and we can hear his call. When that happens, writes Thomas Merton, "We become like vessels empty of water that they may be filled with wine. We are like glass cleansed of dust and grime to receive the sun and vanish into its light."

December, ironically enough, seems to be one of the most difficult times of the year to achieve the "room" in our lives that is so central to the Advent spirit. Who has time to slow down for the spirit of love when there's so much preparation for the holiday to be done?

Happily for us, we don't have to necessarily empty every single moment of Advent to taste the gifts that God can afford. He's merciful; he'll find a way to touch us if we go even partway out to meet him. In fact, my experience confirms that even a few hours may bring that light flooding in.

✥ ✥ ✥

Every year on the afternoon of the First Sunday in Advent three friends and I gather for a wreath-making party at my house. They bring distinctive cuttings to share from their home plantings. One lugs big bags of red-berried yew and soft spruce; another carries branches of flaming orange pyracantha; a third brings a box of long-needled ponderosa pine and its cones. I contribute the blue-fruited juniper and dried wild sunflower heads that grow on my mountainside land. We heap the bounty on card tables in the open front room (a "good room," not a "great room," Ford insisted based on its modest size) and assess. There are always plenty of basic raw materials for everyone, but before we get to work we drive out to a pretty little nature area in the national forest to find embellishments, such as fragrant sagebrush clippings, red willow branches, wild rose hips, and dramatic dried grasses.

We never skip this side trip. The fresh air is welcome after many days indoors; the opportunity to see at close range what the natural world has been up to is instructive. To undertake the jaunt each year on the same day is to engage in an informal but controlled comparative observation of the Intermountain West ecosystem. Often we've walked in hard snow under a clear sky; occasionally a blizzard-in-progress has made the afternoon an adventure. One year the weather felt like September. Some years the Russian olive trees have borne abundant silver-grey fruits; sometimes there are none. Remarking on the bumper crop of indigo Oregon grape berries but sparse snow this year, we discuss global warming.

Back at the house I turn on Christmas music and light the pellet stove, and the afternoon's work commences in earnest. Not-very-expensive champagne is opened; the first homemade cookies and candies, fancy cheeses and crackers and smoked fish of the season are gobbled up. As we attach clippings to straw wreath forms, we gossip and laugh and lose our scissors and strew the floor with pine needles and berries. We make a serious mess and then pitch in collectively to sweep it up. After the work is done we linger by the fireplace to talk some more.

You might say that we waste an entire afternoon together—or that's what we'd probably say, anyway, if we were in any guise but our wreath-making selves. Taking time for an afternoon of crafting might be nice, we'd grant with a hint of condescension, but we just don't have the luxury of such leisure. We're busy women, university professors who must make every minute count and habitually work many hours outside a normal forty-hour Monday–Friday schedule. Sunday afternoons usually find us preparing for the week ahead. We're people who rarely have time to eat lunch or go for walks together. A long time has typically passed before the wreath-making party without any conversation among us except for passing words in the university corridors or the briefest of drop-in visits to each others' offices.

Once we're together, though, we remember why we love each other. Pamela is so wry, regaling us with stories about university politics that inspire gasps of laughter. Janie is so characteristically generous with her yew, her floral pins, and her gentle queries about our families and our endeavors. Catherine, younger than the rest of us by two decades, is so driven, so endearingly serious about her most recent article-in-progress and about the graduate seminar she's teaching. She's a relatively recent addition to the group, invited after an original member moved away. At first she temporized, voicing deep reservations. She "wasn't crafty," she said. We smiled and suggested that she try, and her very first wreath party put that apprehension to rest.

The wreaths that we build on these December Sunday afternoons reflect individual personalities so consistently that if someone missed a party and was presented with the other three specimens she'd instantly know whose was whose. Janie's wreaths are the epitome of comforting and homey, dense with greens and heavily decked with yew berries. Pamela's creations are artistic and experimental; willow and Russian olive branches project from their edges into an airy three-dimensionality. Catherine's wreaths are traditional and precise—they look like an even more elegant version of the ones in *Martha Stewart Living*. Mine are exuberant, decked to a fare-thee-well with blue juniper berries, orange pyracantha, clusters of cones and sagebrush and rosehips. I'm often teased about whether I'm certain that I've included at least a sprig of absolutely everything that everybody has brought.

We've shared troubles as well as laughter at wreath-making parties, though never in the form of the gushing tear-fests that women in the movies appear to find so healing. Instead we talk in gentle code, letting the friend with the misfortune reveal only as much as she chooses. Last year one of us confided that her long marriage was ending. Rather than asking her directly how she felt, we let her choose her own topics, and they revolved around the next phase: how she's coping with the big house she now inhabits alone, her plans to go cross-country skiing with her sister in January, the daily walks she takes with her daughter. She sounded centered and calm, and we were reassured. Only after we settled down by the fire toward the afternoon's end did she allude more directly to her sorrows, insisting that things were better now that the marriage had been dissolved. She felt relief, not increased pain.

Thus we renew our friendships every Advent as we combine pine and sagebrush, juniper and rose hips to welcome the season. In my case the renewal of connection stretches deeper still, for I remember when the tradition began. Almost thirty years ago, back when I was a newly married assistant professor, I learned the technique that my friends and I use today from the wife of the then-department chair. Nan had called seeking a companion in wreath-making, and I'd agreed. At the time I'd thought of her as a person with abundant connections, a spirited civic activist and volunteer whom everybody admired, and I'd wondered why she had reached out to me. Since then I've learned something of her troubles, and I think that she might have been looking for a friendship without a complicated backstory. At any rate she taught me to make wreaths, and we spent an afternoon together every December until her husband took a new job across the country.

When she left I asked three of my friends to join me and the new tradition began. Its shape has been a bit more varied than the annual *tête-à-tête* with Nan. In the past some children have attended—group members' daughters in the interval between when they grew big enough to be trusted with clippers and greening pins and when they reached the stage of adolescence that rendered us boring. More often it's been just four of us. We've kept the gathering small not just because of the size of the space in which we work, but also so we can focus on each other as we focus on the evolving wreaths.

Yet the presence of wreath-makers past is very much with us. Nan has died, and I light a candle for her every year before my friends arrive, thanking her for the gift of this festival. The woman whose place Catherine has taken, now living in upstate New York, often receives a phone call from us at some point during the afternoon. We remember those daughters, now away in graduate school or medical school or married, reminiscing about their childhood wreath-making quirks and hearing from their mothers about what they're doing.

⚬ ⚬ ⚬

On the surface this is a party more about holiday decorating than it is about Advent in a religious sense. Two of the others do not attend church at all; Nan was hostile to organized religion. Still, the very fact that we are shaping wreaths calls to mind implications beyond simple decking of the halls. Circles with no beginnings or ends, wreaths evoke unity, peace, and eternal life. The Greeks called wreaths "diadems," from *diadema*, which means "bound together."

Our wreath-making party certainly re-binds us together every year, reminding us of the joy of inhabiting this small human community, this place where we are known and loved through the rolling years. For me, at least (and I suspect also for Pamela, who always attends the same morning mass as I do before the party), shaping Advent wreaths together also carries the echo of a more comprehensive unity. These wreaths, after all, replicate the bigger Advent wreath introduced into the church shortly after the Reformation, though adopted by Catholics only in the twentieth century. In their venerable symbolism, they remind us of an enduring eternal love that whispers through the human affection we've slowed down to enjoy that day.

⚬ ⚬ ⚬

Even as we share the quiet pleasures of the wreath party, nobody among us has any allusion that this episode of leisurely fellowship is anything more than a fleeting interval. Inevitably we're about to get sucked back into the end-of-semester insanity of university life. We'll be lucky if we get to enjoy even brief commiseration in the hallways during the weeks immediately ahead.

It's good to know, though, that this afternoon is not the last chance we'll have to enjoy each other's company this season. A two-week vacation will follow the end-of-semester chaos. During that precious interval we'll meet regularly, joining with families, friends, and significant others at dinners and parties. On the doors of four of the houses hosting those gatherings will hang welcoming Advent wreaths, each with a very distinctive style, made so long ago (it will seem by then) on a day when we prepared room for one another.

I suspect that I'm not the only one of the four who smiles when she sees these wreaths, these tangible emblems of the love that endures below the fractured surface of our lives.

3

Proclaiming Faith

Putting Up Christmas Lights

I admit it: I'm a Christmas light purist. I do enjoy other people's cheery, even slightly-over-the-top displays—all those colored lights flashing from windows and eves, draped around yard trees and threaded through wire figures of deer or sleighs—though I draw the line at oversized plastic snow globes and dense prefab sheets of icicle lights, especially when they're left up all year. But for my own rural home I've always favored a long single strand of white full-sized bulbs, wound around the deck railing and down the steps to light guests' way to the second-story front door.

Putting up even that restrained display involves more work than it should, in the way of most things Christmas. For some years I've been using LEDs, which offer the advantages of energy savings and safety but the inconvenience of not-quite ideal construction: the plastic "bulbs" that clip over the filaments of each light tend to pop off spontaneously at the slightest provocation. Some fall ten feet through the deck slats to the lawn before the stringing proper has even begun, jostled by the process of untangling the inevitable snarl of cords that has somehow developed inside the big popcorn tins used to store them (the lights were neatly coiled, I'm sure, when I put them away last January). The painstaking process of weaving the strands evenly around the deck's railing dislodges more. Invariably I make three or four trips down the long flight of steps during the decorating process to retrieve the escapees, trying not to cuss, knowing that this is only the beginning of such maintenance during the six weeks these lights will shine. Anything—a wind gust (and the wind gusts often in our canyon), a heavy snow or hail storm, a bird jostling the cord as it lands on a railing, a slight change in barometric pressure that ever-so-slightly relaxes pressure on the plastic fibers—can lead to further truancy. A few of the bulbs don't get retrieved until a summer lawnmower coughs and stalls.

One aspect of Christmas light maintenance is easier than it once was, though: I've finally acquired a timer. When my husband was alive we took turns plugging the display in and out of the deck outlet each night, a tiptoeing, perilous process in icy or snowy weather. The second Christmas after his death I took a bad fall, lay stunned for a few minutes, then realized that the temperature was below zero and forced myself to crawl back into the house. A friend presented me with a package from Radio Shack two days later. Now the lights cycle automatically—on at 5 p.m., off at 11 p.m., on again at 6 a.m. for two hours. I'm especially fond of the morning phase, for my bedroom opens onto the deck and the lights allow me to check the time without looking at the clock. They offer a very gentle alarm clock, these deceptively demanding white lights, softly reminding me that it's time to take up again the sacred work of living.

Christmas lights carry one of the most straightforward of all the metaphors inherent in contemporary Advent customs. "The people who walked in darkness have seen a great light; those who lived in a land of deep darkness—on them a light has shined,"

Isaiah tells us, inviting us to equate Christ's coming with literal illumination (9:2). The star of Bethlehem echoes that congruence, leading searchers to the wellspring of their salvation. When we put up our lights we celebrate our participation in the mystery of the incarnation, taking a stand against the ignorance and sin that darkness symbolizes. We proclaim our faith that despair and fear are only temporary. We affirm our trust that God has not forgotten us, that we will live again after death in glory with him.

Beyond such theological weightiness, the simple physical glow of Christmas lights offers a particular comfort to those of us who live in northern latitudes. In the mountains on the forty-fifth parallel in Idaho where I live, the December sun drops behind the ridges before five p.m. and doesn't break their line to rise again until almost nine in the morning. Christmas lights function as little extensions of the sun, earth-bound stars that help bridge the long blackness between one short day and another. They invite us to anticipate the coming of another day, another, and another.

That sort of bridging took on new poignancy in our suburban Mink Creek neighborhood a few Christmases ago, when we found ourselves much darker than we'd been in the past. The district is what's properly called "urban interface," a place where houses edge into wilderness and wildfires are always a concern. Everyone's worst fears had come true the previous June when flames engulfed the sage- and juniper-covered landscape, fueled by an unprecedented lack of rain, ninety-five-degree temperatures, and 45-mph gusts. Before firefighters stopped the wall of fire it consumed sixty-six homes, many outbuildings, and a thousand acres. In several side canyons only a few dwellings were spared. In others the destruction took an apparently random (and even more disturbing) shape, plucking one home while leaving the one next door untouched. My neighbors and I returned after three days' evacuation to a moonscape punctuated by stark orphaned chimneys.

In retrospect we were collectively lucky—no human died or was even seriously injured, though pets and wildlife suffered. I was individually luckier still. The fire raced through the gully between my next door neighbors' house and mine, up the slope to the edge of my green lawn, lapping just three feet from the deck where I string Christmas lights. At that moment the prevailing wind direction shifted and abruptly sheered the flames away from the house, around the edge of my developed property. Two of the three acres I own did burn—157 junipers, by Allstate's count, went to tree heaven; peripheral plantings and sprinkler piping scorched. Three of my five closest neighbors were burned out. My house remained completely untouched, however, standing as if charmed or blessed on the narrow peninsula of green lawn my husband had nurtured as a firebreak, encircled on three sides by black devastation.

My next door neighbors weren't as fortunate. When winter came that year I realized just how comfortably familiar their house's presence had become—the glow from the kitchen window, the outlines of the hoop house garden under the snow, the line of Christmas lights on the garage. Cleared of wreckage, the space became a blacker void than it would have been had the house never existed.

Those neighbors haven't yet decided if they're going to rebuild. They're renting in town and have discovered that they don't miss the eight-mile commute at all. Other fire victims acted more decisively, putting their properties on the market within a month and buying new homes safely ensconced in urban neighborhoods. One of these told me that she didn't understand how anyone could still want to live in the Mink Creek since the landscape had been "spoiled" by the loss of so many junipers.

The most disturbing cases involved people so paralyzed by their losses that they were unable to imagine a course of action. For a long time after the fire the chimneys and mounds of dank snow-covered ash that were once their homes stood undemolished; the last finally fell to the bulldozer more than two years after the flames were extinguished.

Human beings tend to be resilient creatures, though, and the majority of neighbors who lost their homes soon began to rebuild. Even as the first post-fire December dawned, framed-in houses dotted mountainsides and ridges. A few were so far along that contractors could work snugly inside; the occupants took possession in the spring. Venturing out into my yard to fill bird feeders that Advent, I could hear the thud of hammers and the burr of power tools from a house rising nearby. From some spots on the main road you could see as many as ten under-construction homes at once, and it was a decidedly a cheerful sight. Even more cheerful: driving home after teaching a night class, I noticed a string of Christmas lights draped across the roof line of one work-in-progress.

That winter I strung my own Christmas lights with particular fervor, hoping that the resolute glow of that single strand of ersatz stars shining against a black hillside would make someone else smile. "Take heart," I imagined those lights as saying. "Be cheerful. God has not abandoned us, and we have not abandoned each other. Next year we will shine again in merry company."

That has happened. This year my street and all the others in the Mink Creek neighborhood sparkle, long-standing houses and brand-new ones alike sporting Christmas glory. Some of those displays testify to people like me whose houses survived; others to those who lost their homes but could not imagine abandoning the mountain landscape they loved. Other displays testify to newcomers willing to put their trust in a place already starting to regenerate itself in summer greenery—a place whose glorious sweeping views of summits and stars remain unsullied by the flames, whose deer and moose and ermine (the eponymous "minks" of the Mink Creek) have also returned in great numbers.

Since the wildfire I've been trying to curtail my irritation over the shedding bulbs. Putting the display up isn't much work, nor is going down to that godsend of a lawn, now snow-covered, to retrieve errant little pieces of plastic.

Though the fire and its aftermath have passed, the need for such testimony remains. It's not just in obvious and dramatic catastrophes that human beings need encouragement to persevere.

Looking out across the gleaming deck into evening blackness, down to the road that threads the bottom of the Mink Creek Canyon, I wonder whether some of those headlights represent people even now struggling with personal troubles—difficulties more burdensome for being private, in contrast to the shared communal travail through which my neighbors and I supported each other. Who wouldn't hope to offer a cheerful, literal light to those hearts? And perhaps a bit of more enduring light, too. As a celebration of Christmas, this display represents a sign of trust in God's "steadfast love and faithfulness," in a renewal of eternal life unimaginably more glorious than even the most welcome signs of earthly renewal.

We all need the glow of the Advent promise that Christmas lights represent, in winter's darkness and in the other kinds of dark seasons our lives will hold. "All is not lost," these little points of hope proclaim in the face of mutability and ruin, catastrophe and death. "Join me in affirming that the light will come again."

4

Cultivating Hospitality

Planning a Big Party

By the end of the first week of December it's high time to begin planning a much bigger annual party than the wreath-making fest: the open house I've hosted for three decades on the weekend before Christmas. Though I've learned to enjoy many things about living alone since 2002, Advent seems to call for sociability.

Orchestrating a four-hour event that entails serving substantial hors d'oeuvres and drinks to forty or fifty people involves a great deal of frazzled work, even with a confederate standing in as sous chef. At some point I'll inevitably wonder why on earth I'm putting myself through this effort yet again. Still, like a woman whose memory of childbirth trauma fades in the joy of motherhood, by the time the first guests arrive the second-guessing will be history.

Perhaps I have a genetic or temperamental predisposition for large-scale organizing. There's actually some evidence for the latter. The Myers–Briggs personality inventory test has placed me (in successive results from my twenties through my sixties) squarely in the ENTJ group (extroverted, intuitive, thinking, judging), a configuration of traits nicknamed "The Field Marshall." As is typical of such obsessively-organized people, the logistics of planning big events strike me as less daunting than they appear to others. In this season in particular it seems like somebody HAS to bring people together, and that somebody would be me. Like Virginia Woolf's fictitious character Mrs. Dalloway (and Woolf's sister, upon whom the character is based) in December my heart whispers that providing the occasion for fellowship is essentially a vocation.

ᴥ ᴥ ᴥ

Hospitality is a Christian virtue, one especially relevant to this season. Jesus was unremittingly hospitable to those of good will whom he met, friends and strangers alike. We must, he taught, love our neighbors as ourselves (Luke 10:29-37). The story of Martha and Mary welcoming Christ to their home, which immediately follows the parable of the Good Samaritan (where the above remark about love appears), reinforces that sentiment. The Christmas story offers its own paradigm of hospitality when Mary and Joseph entertain a decidedly odd assemblage of guests from grand to humble around the manger.

Welcoming others is more particularly a central virtue in Benedictine culture, a perspective familiar to me thanks to long association with a community of Benedictine nuns in northern Idaho. A former student lives among them; all have become friends and mentors. I've been visiting annually for at least a week each summer since my husband died, seeking solace at first, more recently renewal and creative inspiration.

The community is familiarly called "St. Gertrude's," and it's a marvelous place for a retreat. Peace infuses the sisters' century-old convent, whose grey-blue stone towers look to the east across the Camas Prairie sixty miles to the Clearwater River Gorge and even more distant mountain ranges. The monastery's retreat house offers sweeping views of that rolling expanse; its rooms and the well-stocked library invite study and reflection. If a person needs a break there are the summer gardens buzzing with hummingbirds and the high wooded hill on which the sisters care for a managed forest. One can find spiritual direction, organized classes, good conversation, merry laughter, and marvelous homemade food.

The sisters' openhearted welcome epitomizes a contemporary version of Benedict's sixth-century call to monastic hospitality. "All guests who present themselves are to welcomed as Christ, for he himself will say: *I was a stranger and you welcomed me* (Matt 25:35)," St. Benedict wrote in his Rule. "Proper honor must be shown to all . . . . Once a guest has been announced, the superior and [the community] are to meet [the guest] with all the courtesy of love."

Since being introduced to the wonderful cheer and acceptance of Benedictine hospitality I've attempted to greet all guests to my own home in the same spirit. As Benedict himself acknowledged, however, extending general welcome in the space where one lives can pose challenges. The Rule cautions that not all visitors will necessarily be on the up-and-up. Benedict instructs monastics to pray with a stranger before extending the kiss of peace (if the visitor is a devil in disguise, this holy gesture will presumably send him fleeing). Even well-intentioned guests can prove distracting, for they may offer frivolous or potentially corrupting discourse that diverts monks' thoughts to the outside world. Benedict prohibited his sixth-century monks "to speak or associate with guests unless they are bidden." The community's leaders and those designated to tend to visitors may converse as necessary, he grants, but ordinary monastics must limit themselves to simple greetings and blessings. Happily for twenty-first-century convent visitors this latter proviso has been revised, and now conversation is general.

Visitors and their schemes and babble aside, according to Benedict even fellow community members can disrupt a monastery's equanimity. Some people *will* be difficult, and extending the daily hospitality of courtesy and filial love to them will pose a challenge. The Rule offers guidance for dealing with a litany of disruptive personality types: "stubborn, disobedient, or proud," grumblers, the habitually tardy, people who do their work haphazardly, those who "lack understanding," those who might be tempted to "excess and drunkenness," those with a tendency toward "idle talk." Specific sanctions for particular offenses are stipulated; the consequences become more severe for habitual misbehavior and end with excommunication from the community, although Benedict does allow mercy and reintegration for those willing to reform.

Some things never change, and human nature is certainly one of them. Fifteen hundred years after Benedict a very similar roster of human peccadillos poses challenges for people today who labor to infuse a cheerful and cooperative ethos into organizations, businesses, families, and classrooms—and for those planning guest lists for large Christmas parties.

First on my own roster this year, as always, are people who embrace the spirit of Benedictine hospitality even though they may not know anything about the saint and his Rule. Among them are dear friends, congenial coworkers, and nice neighbors who make others feel at home. Others with whom I personally get along well, however, pose more vexed decisions. Several have recently disrupted the community of people who will assemble, including the ex-husband of my wreath-making friend. Some are habitually ornery. I consider again as I do every year whether or not I should invite the two feuding colleagues who challenge each other's every suggestion in department meetings. There are a few university administrators whose recent decisions have inspired bitter mumbling among some other potential guests.

What if the crush of space juxtaposes the wrong people in my house? There must be no awkwardness or unpleasantness at the Christmas party.

Others who probably should be invited are socially inept, people whose "idle talk" or lack of social graces threaten to derail conversation. Prominent among them in more ways than one is a man who tends to lecture anyone within earshot about any possible topic of conversation (he's one of those experts on everything). Though including him honors the season's spirit of tolerance and mercy, it will also inevitably compromise others' ease. Some potential guests are more quietly tedious, people who ramble on, free-associating about their lives without appearing to realize that conversation means taking turns and asking questions. Some are so shy that I've stumbled upon them taking breathers in the bedroom with the coats or out on the back porch with the spare beer. Would it be a mercy to spare these introverts this year?

Each year some new strangers are candidates for the guest list— not strangers to me but to the regulars. Over the course of this particular past year I've made new friends in the sciences, mathematics, and engineering. I've met congenial people at church and as a member on various boards. The newly arrived university public information officer and I hit it off. Will these newcomers feel comfortable among people who have known each other forever?

This stranger demographic was particularly robust when my husband was alive, since Ford cultivated a diverse circle of acquaintance. River runners and mountain climbers, NAACP members and union organizers, railroad workers and carpenters, crazed poets and serious musicians often appeared at the party back then. One of my happiest memories from that era involves a dignified Tanzanian priest and a rough-hewn socialist barfly deep in amiable conversation.

The most difficult choices involve potential guests who consider themselves estranged from me. This year only two people (that I know of) fall into that category. One is the wife of a colleague, a woman perennially angry at me for a long-ago decision that affected her husband. He seems to have put our differences behind him long ago and is invariably cordial, but she still attempts to pretend that she does not see me when we run into each other around town. The other is closer to the bone, a woman once among my most intimate friends whom I offended by inconceivably thoughtless speech (*mea culpa*). Confession and apology have done nothing to mollify her resolve for an irrevocable break. I miss her every day.

Will she—and the other angry woman—feel even more aggrieved if they're invited? Will the gesture seem presumptive and pushy? Or will not inviting them confirm in their minds that I'm the reprobate they consider me to be?

ᵅ ᵅ ᵅ

In the end I invite these two as always, and everyone else who is not absolutely dedicated to making trouble. I invite them because conscience whispers that inclusivity is the right thing to do in this season when the liturgy instructs us to be patient and kind, to avoid judging and to forego grumbling about others. It's the disenfranchised and the difficult, after all, who really need hospitality. As Benedict reminds his monastics, "Great care and concern are to be shown in receiving poor people and pilgrims, because in them more particularly Christ is received."

It's hard not to imagine all the things that could go wrong in an assemblage that includes contemporary versions of wise men and shepherds, gentle saints and gleeful sinners, believers and atheists, egotists and altruists, galloping extroverts and retiring introverts. The space is objectively too small for the number of guests; folks will of necessity be squeezed in, perhaps in less-than-ideal juxtapositions.

But I squelch such anxiety (though I know from experience that it will return deep in the nights immediately preceding the party) and stuff the invitations into envelopes, trusting that the gesture will lead to a space that is hospitable, even in its way holy.

It always has. Last year the enemies who turn department meetings into battlegrounds declared a brief truce and sat together in the corner, talking companionably about their research-in-progress. Two of the strangers turned out to be not absolute strangers after all, but decades-ago high school classmates of a pair of party regulars. A dashing new male colleague sought out one of the unattached introverts and something pleasant now seems to be brewing. I myself had a wonderful conversation with a colleague to whom I've never paid much attention. For the past year I've been stopping to share the hospitality of a daily greeting. We have more in common than I imagined.

⚬ ⚬ ⚬

Gazing at the stack of envelopes I reassure myself that the important interpersonal matters will turn out well as always—though the space, admittedly, will be jammed. The party is always boisterous; it's advertised as an open house, but people do not obediently come and go and so moderate their numbers as they're supposed to. They'll come early and stay late, good-humoredly jostling each other for space. The mountains of hors d'oeuvres will be despoiled. Pamela's husband Russell, my late husband's best friend in the department, will stand in the midst of the swirl at the counter cheerfully wielding cocktail shakers and opening bottles, retrieving beer and ice cubes from the frigid back yard as necessary. Others of a helpful disposition will keep an eye out for discarded paper plates and plastic glasses, squeezing through the throng to the laundry room trash can. Conversation will bounce off the ceiling at a deafening pitch (why do I bother to stack Christmas CDs in the changer?). If this iteration is true to form, no one will seem to mind.

I smile, already looking forward to that evening as I stand by a counter now bare except for envelopes, in a "good room" now absolutely serene. It's such a joy to extend this invitation to gather despite our differences in the season's spirit of celebration. It's such a sacred responsibility to be the one, year after year, to whom the task falls of reminding the others that life is infinitely more livable if we extend the "proper honor" (as Benedict puts it) of affectionate, tolerant hospitality to all we meet.

In the quiet of this anticipatory night, another way of saying the same thing suddenly comes to mind, a phrase from one of my late husband's books. The poem begins by recording an encounter with an enormous moose, not a person, but the point soon broadens to suggest a more comprehensive interdependence. If all of us who share this earth are to coexist and nurture the community where we have been placed, Ford suggests in a line that applies to carefully orchestrated gatherings as well as chance encounters, we can do nothing less than attempt to act, always and everywhere, as "guests of one another."

Week 2

Taking Stock Before God

5

Practicing Patience

Managing Seasonal Stress

Early in George Frideric Handel's oratorio *Messiah*, a startling shift in tone brings what has to be one of the great wake-up-call moments in music. The previous parts of the composition have announced the Savior's coming with uplifting words and melodies. The tenor solo has invited universal comfort, and the chorus has proclaimed that "the glory of the Lord shall be revealed. And all flesh shall see it together." There is nothing to fear and everything to celebrate in the Messiah's immanent appearance, as these joyful opening sections suggest.

Then the mood abruptly shifts. A bass soloist alludes to the Lord shaking the earth and the heavens; an alto soloist suggests that as sinners we may not be adequately prepared. "But who may abide the day of his coming, and who shall stand when he appeareth?" she asks, likening God's judgment to a "refiner's fire." The dramatic, dark chorus that follows conjures up purification's fearsome flames.

That progression has always seemed to me a painfully accurate representation of what experiencing Advent in the real world feels like. In common with the voices that begin Handel's great work, it's so natural for us to be swept up in excitement as the season dawns; it's so easy to vow exemplary observance in preparing the way of the Lord.

Actually honoring those vows in the face of December's seasonal stress is something else entirely. Crowds in stores, heavy traffic, and winter weather complicate ordinary errands as well as Christmas preparations. Stress hormones like cortisol flood our systems. Such "fight or flight" hormones make us edgy if not outright hostile to those with whom we are competing for space and passage. Medical professionals report that the majority of people report fatigue and anxiety during the Christmas season; many feel depression. So well-documented is the connection between seasonal stress and illness that no less an authority than the American Heart Association puts holiday-stress-beating tips on its website.

We are liable to many kinds of "heart trouble," in fact, during Advent's busy weeks. It's very difficult to cultivate altruism or sacred contemplation when you're irritated with others, pressed for time, and aggrieved. It's so easy to forget the noble intentions of early Advent.

What's especially discouraging is to realize that you've slipped into such bad behavior before December has even reached double digits.

⋗ ⋗ ⋗

The first two weeks of Advent in my world also hold the final days of the university's fall semester—an end-time that doesn't need the addition of seasonal stress to bring out the worst in everybody. Obsessive students dicker about grades; desultory ones reappear after months of absence and ask, "Did I miss anything?"

Graduate teaching assistants tearfully doubt their vocation and require immediate counseling at the most inopportune moments. Piles of long papers demand careful comments; exams must be composed and final grades figured; reports and self-evaluations come due.

Several Decembers ago my plate was even fuller. In addition to all of the above, I'd been cajoled into both chairing the university general education committee and directing the English composition program. The first assignment meant defending responsible decisions to outside parties possessed of veto power and hostile agendas. The second dictated that I act as designated adjudicator for all end-of-semester plagiarism cases in all the English department's myriad writing courses. Constant snow slowed the commute from home to campus; a conference paper deadline loomed; a book review was overdue. Shopping and decorating became low priorities. As of the second Sunday in Advent I'd sent no cards, bought no tree, planned no menu for the Christmas party. Spiritual observance of the season had slipped. I barely remembered what prayer was and had been seriously tempted to skip Mass in favor of grading on Sunday mornings. Only the music kept me faithful.

Adrenaline makes a lousy diet. That year cutting off others in traffic had become business-as-usual (*Get a life, people!!*). I mounted a high horse when students offered excuses for late papers, even legitimate excuses (*I do MY work when I have a cold!!*). I snapped at a friend when she suggested that we go cross-country skiing. I pushed past colleagues when conversations at the mailbox impeded progress and slammed the office door when a cluster of graduate students across the hall was having too much fun.

Then somebody called me on such uncivil, self-important behavior—an angel in the shape of a supermarket checker. The revelation happened while I was waiting in line after work, chafing to get home and wolf down premade fried chicken and deli salads as quickly as possible so that I could get on with the evening's obligations.

Life had come to a screeching halt, however. An elderly woman stood in front of me, slowly (SO S-L-O-W-L-Y) loading items from her full cart one at a time onto the belt, pausing every two or three items to chat with the cashier.

"My son and his family are coming for Christmas from Utah this year," she announced, enumerating her myriad grandchildren's names and ages.

"You must be so excited about seeing them, Hon." The clerk smiled.

"Oh, yes!" The woman lifted one lemon from her cart, ignoring the other three. "Did I tell you he's a lawyer?"

Waiting carts stretched to block an entire aisle. "Why don't they open another line?" I asked the man behind me, a little more loudly than necessary. I tapped my foot. I picked up my fried chicken as if the second I'd spend lifting it from the cart when my turn came was precious. I transitioned to glaring, then to eye-rolling. I muttered "Abandon hope" and shook my head as yet another person joined our line.

Eventually the old woman trundled off toward her car. I threw my groceries onto the belt and placed an already signed check on the writing platform as items began cycling through, tapping a pen in anticipation of the total.

"Twelve-twenty-four," the cashier said very quietly as the last item cleared. As she took my check, she gathered herself and held my eyes. "She's so lonely," she said without bothering to supply the referent. "Someday we might be there, too."

Then she wheeled away from me to face the next person, her tone abruptly casual and bright. "Who's next? Come on down!"

⚬ ⚬ ⚬

Reconciliation, anyone? Despite a calendar I'd believed overfull, the next afternoon found me in spiritual E.R. Our Vietnamese priest Fr. Dat listened patiently as I wept out my shame. "I can't watch and wait for God for fifteen minutes. I'm failing Advent."

The always-compassionate Dat consoled me—up to a point. Certainly I was busy, and a lot of that work couldn't be avoided. But yes, it was time to check the attitude.

"So," he announced, "For your penance I'm going to *add* something to your to-do list."

Oh no. How many thousand Hail Marys?

What Father Dat prescribed—a customized riff on the familiar practice of random acts of kindness—was at once simpler and more daunting. For the remainder of Advent I was instructed to do not just something nice but something specifically *patient* each day. Saint Paul, he reminded me, included patience in the list of qualities essential for a Christian. "With all humility and gentleness, with patience, bearing with one another in love," he read aloud from the Bible beside him (Eph 4:2). If I could learn to wait a few minutes for others without griping, Fr. Dat assured me, I'd be honoring a God who is always patient with us. If I could allow myself to trust that there would be enough time and space for all of us and I didn't have to grab my share, I'd be affirming the expansive inclusivity of God's love. "Think of patient things," Fr. Dat concluded, "as gifts for the Baby Jesus. Imagine you're making an Advent calendar. Put some nice little surprise behind the door every day that will make him smile when he opens it up."

⌖ ⌖ ⌖

What did I give Him, poor as I was?

December 8: When a random student loomed in the office door and asked, "Where's Professor Smith's office?" I didn't snap (without looking up from my work), "There's a bulletin board by the department office!"

Instead I walked him down the hall to the directory, helped him find the number, and led him to the correct wing of the building.

December 9: When the cars ahead of me took their sweet time responding to a green light, I did not beep. I used the spare twenty seconds to thank God for the wonder of icy branches glistening in the sun's rising light.

December 10: When a young colleague caught me in the hall and confessed that she felt physically threatened by one of those plagiarists, I didn't put her off until a convenient time. I got my coat. I treated at the coffee shop as we made a plan for insuring both her safety and fair treatment for the student.

Potential gifts for the Baby Jesus were everywhere. I'd just been oblivious.

⌖ ⌖ ⌖

Six days into the practice I was challenging myself to present two gifts a day, though the worries about time persisted (*If I lose this moment, I'm not going to be able to get that done*). I also noticed other kinds of anxieties. Sometimes I paused on the verge of pleasing the Baby Jesus to worry about judgment (*People are going to be think I'm slacking off if I'm late*), to confront envy (*Nobody's ever done this for me*), and to fret about the consequences of dropping my boundaries (*Is that woman going to think I'm a sucker?*).

But I was bound to honor my penance and fought these demons down. And I began to notice a remarkable thing: I still had plenty of time and energy for the requisite duties. Actually, time seemed to be *expanding*. One morning I "frittered away" a whole seven minutes helping the department secretary sort an inordinate amount of mail and packages into mailboxes. It had seemed impossible that I'd check everything off my to-do list that day, but by 3 p.m. I adjourned guiltlessly to the Christmas tree lot. My blood pressure dropped even as I woke with more energy, eager to see when the day's opportunity for human sympathy might arise. Those episodes began to seem like happy Advent calendar surprises not just for the Baby Jesus, but also for me.

⚘ ⚘ ⚘

I wish I could say that one Advent was enough to break the old bad habits, to burn away impatience and self-importance. I wish I could truthfully say that forbearance is now second nature.

I can't, however. That first year the Baby Jesus received gifts reliably through January and sporadically into Lent, but by early April the practice had lapsed. In subsequent years it's occasionally reached into mid-May. By summer, however, the discipline has without exception faded to a memory of a more righteous time.

Who may abide the day of his coming, indeed? The only thing to do is to dust oneself off and begin again, trusting that eventually practice will make better if not perfect.

And so this year, as always, as the season's initial vows start to slip I call to mind the image of an Advent calendar with an expression of patience behind each door. Though the days ahead hardly have a chance of being irritation free, the exercise definitely helps in cultivating a less selfish approach to the world.

⟶ ⟶ ⟶

Please note that I use the word "exercise" deliberately in this context; Father Dat's informal prescription shares crucial goals with the better-known "official" spiritual exercises. Granted, the former involves action in the world, not a thirty-day period of solitude, prayer, and highly structured meditation like the famous spiritual exercises of St. Ignatius of Loyola. Still, like that rigorous discipline this humble one encourages a deeper relationship with God. As with Loyola's practice, this one also fosters discernment between the good and vexed spirits that shape the daily character of the Christianity that one is living.

Beyond such weighty fruit, following Fr. Dat's regime is also, frankly a daily pleasure. It's such an easy yoke. Even after long familiarity I feel happily curious each morning about what invitation to patience will present itself in the following hours.

Today's opportunity involved simultaneously opening an Advent calendar door and an actual metal door as I held the latter at the post office for a young mother with three clinging, fretting children.

I paused before following her in to the line, marveling at how automatic the gesture had been on this particular day in Advent. *Practice makes at least better*, I told myself—and for a moment I fancied that I heard the laughter of a baby (not one of hers) ringing at the surprise, faintly and at a great distance in the winter air.

6

Examining Conscience

Writing a Christmas Letter

I'm old enough to remember when nearly all Christmas cards, delivered twice a day in December during my childhood so as not to overburden the mail carriers, came with handwritten personal notes. When the first photocopied generic "Christmas letters" showed up, stuffed into cards that bore only a signature (or not), my parents considered them a tacky shortcut.

How times have changed! Today the cards I receive routinely include letters detailing fantastic vacations, prestigious promotions and honors, beautiful new homes or redecorations, children's attractiveness and fabulous accomplishments, accounts of domestic bliss and of wonderful times with others I've never met. They're illustrated in glorious photos thanks to the wonders of digital technology.

While one is of course glad for one's friends' happiness, in the aggregate such letters can be depressing. Everybody else has such a perfect life, it seems. Why am I missing out? What's wrong with me?

It's hard not to get sucked into such an increasingly widespread custom. After holding out for a long time, even my late husband

and I sent template Christmas letters. We began when Ford was first diagnosed with cancer and so many people wanted to know exactly the same things: the status of his illness, how he was responding to treatment, the prognosis. We told the truth as gently as we could, emphasizing our resolute hope, his continued good spirits, and our appreciation of their concern.

Too exhausted the Christmas after he died to write individual notes but knowing that friends would want to hear from me, I too produced a generic letter. That first winter mine maintained the filtered honesty of those we'd crafted together, but soon I allowed myself to get sucked into standard Christmas letter rhetoric. Believing that I could not admit to continued depression, I sought to reassure correspondents by painting an exaggeratedly happy picture of all the healthy things I was doing: skiing and preparing for half marathons again, beginning a research fellowship, working on articles or books already accepted for publication, planting a rose garden, going to Italian language school.

"I'm glad you're doing so well, but reading your letter made me tired." This reply from a friend across the continent jolted me. In fact the year had been very rocky; I was mired that Advent in the phase of grief where I so badly needed Amy Grant's Mary. While not fantasies, the recounted adventures actually constituted brief, few-and-far-between bright days.

Ashamed, I decided to end the arms race then and there. No more exaggeration. If I were going to continue to write Christmas letters, I needed to give a more honest picture, letting my friends into at least some of the complexity of the immediate past rather than reflexively reaching with the keyboard for the shiniest positive things.

When I tried to honor this intention the following December, however, I realized that I had little idea of the actual day-to-day contours of the preceding year. I sat down with my twelve-month appointment calendar and my journal to jog memories. I forced myself to look beyond the big accomplishments to the rhythms of routine human interactions. I relived the worries and fears and recalled the little moments of satisfaction at work done well, the intervals of hard-won contentment. I dipped back into archived Facebook posts, saved email strings, and even copies of teaching evaluations.

What I discovered surprised me. On the positive side: I'd been a much more giving person during the past year than I imagined. On the insight side: though the shiny things had indeed been satisfying, it was often the daily preparation for them—the routine runs that led to the successful race, the messy process of drafting a manuscript—that had provided the most tangible, enduring joy. On the take-notice side: the separation from community I'd so often felt had been born in the stories I'd been telling myself (*I'm too tired to go to that gathering, and nobody wants to see me anyway*). Those records also held hard news about spiritual life. The aspirations and responses to events recorded in journal entries chronicled a stubborn struggle to force the future into a particular shape and consequent despair when reality proved recalcitrant. They revealed a woman who had forgotten that God moves in mysterious ways and was attempting to steer her own life with a death-grip on the wheel.

I wrote a very different Christmas letter that year, one that gave a more balanced account of the everyday pleasures and of the ongoing, open-ended evolution of my new circumstances.

I admitted the persistence of grief and asked friends for their continued prayers. So many people responded to that letter with so much affection—and with the reassurances I'd been craving but hadn't received when I constructed those I've-got-it-all-together letters.

❧ ❧ ❧

Taking stock is a time-honored practice at the end of a year—or at the beginning of one, as the church encourages in Advent reconciliation. Catholics' understanding of the nature of the latter scrutiny, though, is different than it once was. In the past the faithful thought of confession legalistically, as "satisfaction for sin" (in the words of the Council of Trent), a quasi-judicial process that involved admitting to errors and expiating them through the performance of penances. Printed guides for the examination of conscience offered (and still offer) lists of sins to jog the penitent's memory. The emphasis in this approach, as theologian Tad W. Guzie wrote after Vatican II, is "more on sins than sinfulness, acts rather than attitudes"; the experience becomes one that deals "with symptoms rather than the real disease," which is the individual's core separation from God.

Though I converted long after Vatican II, I was given one of those examination-of-conscience guides to prepare for my first confession and used it assiduously for years. What resulted, I see now, was a sort of anti-Christmas letter to God, a recitation of the highlights of bad behavior. Missing mass on purpose? Check (*I've been giving to others all week, even yesterday. I just need this one day to myself*). Bearing false witness and leading others into sin? Check (*Oh, that delicious gossip!*). Coveting? Check (*only every happily married person I know*). Honoring other gods? Check (*I'm oh-so proud of my reputation at the university as someone who can get things done).* Greed? Check *(that money for the new car could have been given to the parish building fund).* And so on. I always felt guilty when the priest dispensed just a penance of prayer, imagining that I should be metaphorically breaking rocks in the hot sun to work off all the malfeasance.

But the sacrament is now called "reconciliation," and for a reason whose richness runs deep. Now the church interprets confession as a celebration of God's ever-present mercy, of the grace that has led us back to seek him. "The inmost change of heart under the influence of God," Pope John Paul II termed reconciliation in a post-Vatican II exhortation. This perspective on the sacrament emphasizes that God's love has been present all along, though we must still be sorry and do penance. Indeed, in the very experience of being moved to come to a sincere confession—one where we are honest about our struggles and doubts, about the systemic separation from God that we've been feeling—we see him at work in our lives.

What freedom that new perspective gives! Understanding that we do not and cannot earn God's freely-given, never-failing love, we're invited simply to open our hearts to him. How wonderful it is to imagine being known so thoroughly and loved so completely in spite of our faults.

So many of us are afraid of being known, convinced that our fundamental imperfections and weaknesses make us unlovable to God and to each other (and to ourselves). That's one of the reasons, I think, why so many of us surround ourselves with shining fortresses of accomplishment in our Christmas letters, even as the opposite impulse to castigate ourselves with a terrible litany of failures inspires self-doubt.

Reconciliation tells a different story, one of forgiveness and abiding love. Rather than requiring us to grovel in fear, it invites us to encounter ourselves with contrition, yes, but also with confidence in God's essential, unshakeable mercy. He's always loved us, the sacrament insists; he's always been looking forward to our prodigal return. Facing ourselves—and forgiving ourselves, and beginning again in a new spirit—becomes much more possible with that knowledge.

⊶ ⊶ ⊶

Every December the mailbox still swells with cards bearing triumphant lists of achievements and images of people frolicking on beaches, posing with perfect children, and attending perfect weddings.

I'm still writing revisionist Christmas letters, however, as I have ever since that good and honest friend awakened me. This year's correspondence does convey its share of happy news; deluging friends with confessional angst and sad events would be as self-serving as racking up triumphs, as partial and false a picture of the complicated spirit of the year just past. I tell them about a glorious roll-your-own writer's retreat by the ocean this past spring break and about a challenging autumn hike completed in good style. I announce that I've decided to retire in a year and have started taking classes toward a new vocation. After more than three decades of working with my head, I'm going to see if I can work with my hands as a massage therapist for the elderly, the bereaved, caregivers, and cancer patients. I also admit to a new male "friend" in my life, a man I've started seeing two or three nights a week in a finite and grown-up arrangement. H (he considers his given name "Harrison" too grand and goes by just the initial) is very different than Ford—not an intellectual or artist or academic, but a man who has made his life working in the out-of-doors as a guide. Nevertheless his company is proving very congenial. "This is nice," I write to my friends. "I've never been in a relationship like this, but it's working for both of us."

In addition to high points the letter chronicles modest, quirky pleasures (watching kestrel babies born near the house learn to fly, writing original knitted lace patterns for the local yarn shop). It admits to stumbles and anxieties, though I've tried to make the former sound funny and to be judicious in disclosure about the latter. I've even dared to talk a little about faith, though I imagine certain acquaintances shaking their heads—*she's falling for that in her old age; too bad.*

It would have been unthinkable to write any other kind of letter after the recent night when I sat by the fire with my planner, my journals, and my laptop. A glass of wine also stood at hand, for this annual ritual is not a gloomy occasion, though touched by penitence. Saying a little prayer for an honest spirit of inquiry, I attempted to summon both frankness and compassion, to look for the deeper whys of cause and not just the whats of external signs.

Not everything that I learned has appeared in the Christmas letter, nor should it. But many of the revelations will inform the Advent reconciliation pending in a few days.

"In the wilderness prepare the way of the Lord, make straight in the desert a highway for our God" a familiar Advent reading from Isaiah proclaims (40:3). What a life-giving invitation to reconcile with the divine!

And how good it can be to heed the inextricably entwined call to get "straight" with ourselves in this great season of preparation.

7

Reconsidering What's Important

De-Cluttering the Pantry

Housekeeping is not one of my strong suits. For many years I cleaned only sporadically, when people were coming over or when conditions slipped below tolerable. Though the public spaces stayed relatively uncluttered, if you looked closely at the baseboards, ran your fingers over the sink basin, or opened the door to the study, guilty evidence proclaimed that I was a woman with other priorities. I'd much rather read or hike or cook or garden in my spare time, I've always said, than do housework.

Conditions have improved thanks to a young mother who comes to clean every few weeks. A university acquaintance, Blair confessed that she longed to enroll her daughter in Montessori school but couldn't afford tuition. Did I know anyone who might be looking for help? I'd never previously thought of myself as the sort of person who employed a cleaning lady, but in that moment I became one.

A sparkling house greets me when I get home at 5 p.m. on cleaning days; I walk from room to room marveling at how Blair accomplished such miracles in three hours. Though I know that before long mail will stack up on the counters and dust will appear on the furniture, the experience is reminiscent of returning with newly cleaned teeth from the dentist's office.

Even with my young friend's help, unfortunately, some chores necessarily remain mine. One that's particularly challenging is keeping order in closets and drawers; in such hidden spaces the old bad tendency toward negligent housekeeping persists.

Eventually the burgeoning chaos becomes insufferable even to such as me, inspiring periodic overhauls. Among them is the annual de-cluttering of the small pantry closet off the kitchen. This ritual always occurs during Advent's second week, and the timing is not accidental. Much cooking looms, and it cannot be accomplished with joy or efficiency if that storage space is so crammed that maneuvering or finding something specific becomes impossible. Compatriots will join me in the kitchen to cook during the holidays, and they cannot be allowed to glimpse the disarray into which the pantry has fallen.

Weeding out the pantry requires a full afternoon's labor. Everything must be removed from the shelves, inventory taken, and decisions made about what to keep and how to reorganize. The whole space must be scrubbed down. Mental toughness is required. In common with the greater obligation to reconciliation that shares the second week of December in our parish, this domestic sacrament requires a touch of ruthless refiner's fire if the dysfunctional, the obsolete, and the just-plain-unnecessary are to be purged.

～✧～ ～✧～ ～✧～

I edge into the narrow opening (yes, there are things stored on the floor), and for a moment the accumulation of stuff inspires thoughts of procrastination. The situation will not improve by itself, however, so I steel myself and address one shelf at a time, stacking the contents on the kitchen counter into toss or keep piles. I check expiration dates and recollections of when items were purchased. I sniff spices for freshness. The culling begins.

How could I let this happen? Why don't I straighten up in here more often? Shame reddens me—I'm so wasteful when so many people go hungry! This accumulation, I tell myself, is just like the one that cluttered the kitchen of my childhood (a condition I vowed never to replicate). Popular wisdom on hoarding whispers its ugly message: people accumulate unreasonable amounts of stuff because they feel empty and insecure. Maybe this pantry reflects such inner pathology.

But there's work to be done, and as I take up individual items they trace more nuanced choices of cause and effect. I find the jar of lemon curd, purchased back in the spring for Easter pastries I never got around to making. The year was fresh and unseasonably warm then; the crabapple tree blushed pink, narcissus bloomed. My friends Beth and Brian and I led the music at the Easter Vigil; guests came the next day to eat dinner on the lawn. To discard this jar (even though it didn't actually play a part in the festivities) feels like shutting the door on those memories, those harbingers of summer joy.

Other packages reveal failed intentions for healthy eating (kale powder—really?) or culinary experiments (a big bag of the Middle Eastern spice blend za'atar). Soup varieties I never eat bear sale stickers, tagging me as a woman who falls for bargains because they are bargains (I always say that I feel sorry for such people). Open packages of chocolate chips and dried coconut, much the worse for air, testify to distraction and carelessness.

Turning to reach the basket of tea bags, I brush against a half-full bottle of molasses balanced on the edge of a lower shelf (it's one of three, purchased because I'd forgotten about the others). It tumbles to the floor and the imperfectly closed lid pops off. The afternoon suddenly becomes much longer.

Hours later the job is finally finished and I stand in the pantry door regarding neat groupings of like items on clean shelves. Two boxes on the kitchen counter hold commodities bound for the local food bank. Two garbage bags bulge with stale food. I've consolidated the remaining partial bottles of molasses into one and combined partial boxes of whole wheat spaghetti. I've discarded terminally old though initially expensive cookie decorating sugars and royal icing faux flower toppers. I've made lists of what's on hand and what needs to be replaced. A small cluster of items (including the lemon curd) sits on the counter in front of the toaster, deliberately in the way. If I haven't used them in two weeks, they're gone, too.

I breathe easier looking at the uncluttered space. Everything feels pure and open. The idea of cooking—or doing just about anything, in fact—seems full of energy-inspiring promise once more. I'm not going to miss any of the discarded food. In fact, it's already hard to remember exactly what's in those garbage bags. I feel like I've just taken a very long bath and lost twenty pounds.

� � �

"Every increased material possession loads us with new weariness," nineteenth-century English philosopher and critic John Ruskin wrote, a sentiment for which I can vouch on completing the day's chore. Though written in a style less elegant than Ruskin's, a recent run-away bestseller, Marie Kondo's *The*

Life-Changing Magic of Tidying Up, expands on much the same theme. Kondo offers a system for discarding excess possessions and organizing the remainder; she insists that decluttering produces transformative psychological results. Owning too many things saps our time and distracts our attention, Kondo explains, because we must spend time cleaning and tending our belongings. As possessions pile up, they cause stress because we can't remember what we own and can't find what we are looking for (exhibit A: my pantry). We feel wasteful, guilty, stuck in fundamental ways.

The concept that accumulation can burden us not just psychologically and physically but also in a spiritual sense is a venerable one, reaching across centuries and religious traditions. Wise ones including Buddha, Mahatma Gandhi, Hindu sages, and Old Testament prophets have held that material belongings limit our freedom to seek and follow the divine. If we want to focus on what's important, they tell us, we'd better commit to traveling light.

Jesus emphasizes the same point. "Take care! Be on your guard against all kinds of greed," he tells his disciples, "for one's life does not consist in the abundance of possessions." He evokes the birds of the air and the wildflowers that trust in God for sustenance, advising those who seek salvation to sell their belongings and give alms to the poor. Rather than accumulating earthly treasure, we should strive to become "rich toward God" (Luke 12:15-34). He warns the disciples that following him means committing to austerity. "Foxes have holes, and birds of the air have nests, but the Son of Man has nowhere to lay his head" (Matt 8:20).

In the stories we hear at Mass during Advent it is most often people of extremely limited means who encounter the divine, including shepherds, carpenters, fishermen, and beggars. The

Virgin Mary calls herself lowly in the *Magnificat* and notes that God has "filled the hungry with good things, and sent the rich away empty" (Luke 1:53). We are advised that wealthy folks like the rich young man who cling to their hoard of belongings will find following God virtually impossible.

The long tradition of Christian aestheticism demonstrates what it might be like to put such an ethos into practice. Desert Fathers (and Mothers) retired to wild places and unimaginably impoverished circumstances with the intention of seeking God; later saints disciplined themselves by sleeping on bare floors or planks (when they slept) and eating sparsely. Catholics who serve the needy have routinely emphasized that personal austerity and the pursuit of justice for the oppressed go hand in hand. "If you have two coats, one of them belongs to the poor," said the twentieth-century American social activist and nominee for sainthood Dorothy Day. While lay Catholics seldom go as far as such heroic figures, Advent, like Lent, reminds us that we ought to discard the things that come between us and seeking God, including a dazzling array of redundant possessions.

It would be absolutely wonderful to live like this all the time, I tell myself, turning from a pot of formerly canned tomatoes (flavored with za'atar) stewing into soup to glance at the now-orderly pantry. Understand that I'm not fooling myself: we're a long way from the birds of the air here. The space still holds three kinds of chocolate for holiday baking and enough pasta for a month's worth of meals. Even *having* a pantry testifies that I'm what Hindus would call a "householder," a person preoccupied with the things of this world.

Nevertheless the afternoon's experience has inspired thoughts of more comprehensive paring down. As dinner cooks I ponder not just additional physical decluttering (the basement?) but also non-material ways of exchanging heavy burdens for light ones.

Simplifying current responsibilities at work and as a volunteer seems a likely place to begin. Which of those obligations that clutter my days are *really* obligatory, essential for serving students, colleagues, friends, or strangers? Which demand the unique gifts I bring at this particular point in life, and which can be delegated? Which have simply accrued or merely feed the ego?

I've been operating on autopilot for a long time. In the fleeting and precious later days of a long and comfortable career, it will be good to consider what necessary work remains undone. It will be good, too, to ask more general questions about my values and spiritual priorities, to examine whether any comfortable assumptions about who I am and what's important bear expired shelf-dates.

"I'm heavily laden, Lord," I admit in prayer. "Help me find the courage to discard the things I do not need. Help me to unburden myself in all aspects of my life. Help me to travel light into the future, to make space for you."

8

Honoring Holy Silence

Spending an Afternoon Alone Outdoors

Therefore, I will now allure her,
    and bring her into the wilderness,
    and speak tenderly to her.
    —Hosea 2:14

This is my Father's world,
And to my listening ears
All nature sings, and round me rings
The music of the spheres.
This is my Father's world.
I rest me in the thought
Of rocks and trees, of skies and seas;
His hand the wonders wrought.
    —"This Is My Father's World," Maltbie D. Babcock (1901)

"Downloading 53 of 53 messages," the crawler at the bottom of my iPhone announces.

This onslaught hardly seems fair. It's only 6 a.m. on a Saturday, pitch dark outside, and I'm still in bed. All I wanted was to check the weather before going to my desk, where the set of papers due back to students at Tuesday's final exam waits.

Who sends emails in the middle of the night? Fortunately most of the entries are inconsequential advertisements and announcements. Two correspondents, however, sound a more urgent note.

"Call me now or first thing in the morning if you've already gone to bed," a committee member writes. "I'm having trouble getting these bylaw revisions written. Here's a rough draft, and I need your comments stat."

"I HAVE to come in and talk with you on Monday," pleads a student who has amassed two weeks' worth of absences from my composition class. She's also missed both required conferences and failed to submit three major assignments, including the current one. "I'm free between eight and nine in the morning. It's about getting an extension on that paper, the one that was due last week? And when can I turn in the others? I'll see you then."

"No, no, NO!" I pronounce these words aloud with such emphasis that three cats scatter off the bed.

This weekend is dedicated to grading and preparing for Christmas, not reading lengthy new documents or negotiating with a deadbeat. Even during the regular semester office hours were not held at eight a.m. on Monday. Today's schedule has been tightly planned: three hours of work, a quick break for brunch, three more hours of work, then local Christmas cards.

Every now and then I muster the gumption to say no (or at least "later"), and this is one such occasion. "Thanks. Busy with end of semester, but will try Wednesday," I fire back to the colleague, pleased with the telegraphic style's implication. "I can't see you Monday," I reply to the student. "Check the syllabus and final assignment policies—last Wednesday was the absolutely last date to turn in late papers. If you still want to talk, we'll make a time after the final."

I stick to my guns very satisfactorily through the morning, ignoring the telephone when it rings and the ever-burgeoning email list. So righteous is my indignation at those who would trespass that grading morphs symbolically into an expression of autonomy (that's a first!). The morning session stretches for four hours, not three.

After a sandwich, though, rebellion flares. The well of disciplined concentration is dry; irritation has returned. This is no state in which to evaluate student work or to interact with anybody. What I need most today, my soul whispers, is to step aside from the noise and reclaim the peace that is the season's essence. The task on the desk will get done somehow and new tasks will accumulate. But it won't always be Advent.

That's how I find myself at 1:30 on a brilliantly sunny Saturday December afternoon strapping on snowshoes at a national forest trailhead. I haven't brought the iPod; any words, even those from the songs on the Advent playlist, feel like too much at the moment. I'm here seeking inner stillness, outer silence. Not just any silence, though. This afternoon I'm hoping to bask in a contemplative and calming sense of God's presence in the natural world—a phenomenon celebrated in my favorite childhood hymn (I was a little Presbyterian then) and encountered on myriad occasions since.

As a person who lives happily alone, you might imagine that I'd be an expert at contemplation. Instead I'm endowed with a vigorous "monkey mind," to use the Buddhist trope for obsessive, restless cognition. I'm almost always thinking in words, looping through worries, analysis, memories, and projections. Attempting to sit still and deliberately cultivate a meditative state puts those monkeys into defiant overdrive.

It's not that I'm hostile to the idea of contemplation. The evidence of its physical, emotional, and spiritual benefits is extensive and convincing. I've attempted Zen meditation, and I've studied the parallel Christian practice, contemplative prayer. The latter, promulgated by Cistercian monk Thomas Keating, involves sitting silently still with one's eyes closed and focusing on a sacred word like "Jesus" or "Abba." Practicing in this way for at least twenty minutes a day, it is said, brings "communion rather than conversation" with God. I know several people who affirm that Christian contemplative prayer has immeasurably deepened their relationship with the divine. I just wish I were among them.

Rather than fruitlessly fighting a fidgety nature, I've learned to work with my mind as it is. Instead of attempting to sit still in the pursuit of inner quiet, I cultivate calm receptivity by moving (ideally outdoors), paying attention to each step and taking in the external world as it comes. Only recently did I learn that this technique has a name: "walking meditation." When the term was introduced at a yoga retreat it sounded exotic, but as our leader guided us through the practice I felt a rush of recognition. I'd been doing walking meditation for years during innumerable past hikes and runs, it turned out, letting thought dissolve of its own accord into the simple peace of putting one foot in front of the other, into the calming focus on rocks and trees, skies and seas.

❧ ❧ ❧

A mile into the six-mile loop I turn east up the narrow canyon that holds Blind Springs. Rocky granite palisades close in as the trail climbs; the creek dances and sparkles under broken ice. It's time for a temporary return to conscious attention: mountain lion tracks often appear in this vicinity. A big cat may be watching from a sunny ledge on the hillside or a thick brushy copse of juniper and sagebrush across the creek.

I'm not too worried, however. I'm carrying pepper spray. I look nothing like a deer. The cats are hunted in the fall and wary of humans; they make themselves scarce if you announce your presence. My snowshoes certainly do that, crunching on the hard surface of old snow. Just to be sure, every time I approach a bend I call "Hi, Critters! It's just me!"

Some people, I'm aware, would consider a solo expedition in such wild country irresponsible. Outdoor recreation literature advises against hiking alone; friends chide me for doing so. "Aren't you scared out there?" they ask. "It's so deserted. Aren't you tempting fate?" Perhaps. But solitary passage through a remote landscape offers incomparable gifts. When I'm alone in such places I almost imagine that I can feel emanations in particular spots. Moments of insight or comfort come spontaneously. Even the most congenial hiking companions (and I count several) constitute a distraction. Walking with them is delightful, but it's another kind of experience, an interlude of social interaction that happens to take place in nature. Alone, one is free to concentrate on the land itself; one feels more actually in the place. "Acceptable risk," I tell those anxious friends.

Being no fool I nevertheless keep my eyes peeled, keep calling through the canyon's upper stretch to whatever might be watching. And I do breathe easier, admittedly, when the trail bends south into more open ground and I reach the bottom of the hill that climbs to the plateau.

The first stretch is quite steep. I place the snowshoes' crampons just so to avoid a nasty slip; I slow the pace when breathing becomes labored. Halfway up I stop beside a cluster of aspens, silver skeletons against the sky's bright cerulean. A flock of Rocky Mountain chickadees—those most lively and cheerful birds—darts among the branches. "Dee-dee-DEE!" they call, and I return the greeting aloud. It's impossible not to grin at them, to linger and watch their play, and I do.

Finally the trail breaks out onto the high meadow below Scout Mountain's west face, plastered in snow. Large hoar-frost crystals edge the path, sparkling brilliantly in the sun's lowering angle. I stop again, bending to gather a small handful and bring them to my mouth, then turn slowly 360 degrees to take in the mountain ranges that ring the horizon, some near, some fifty miles distant. These are well-known, beloved home mountains; I've stood on most of their summits. I cycle through their names as if saying the decade of a rosary, wishing them peace, thanking God for the gift of living in this place.

Then it's on along a gentle rolling mile, following the trail through open fields and stands of pines, enjoying the easy rhythm of steps and breath. When I reach the steep descent that signals the second half of the loop and must again pay attention to footing, I realize that my mind has been empty of articulate thought for many minutes. The morning's anxiety and resentment have completely disappeared, dissolved into a pervading sense of peace.

❧ ❧ ❧

Though the concept of outdoor walking meditation might strike some conservative Christians as having pagan, nature-worshipping overtones, there's abundant biblical precedent for finding clarity, renewal, even contact with the divine in "deserted" country. Moses hears God's voice in a burning bush; he learns God's name and receives his call to lead Israel on a mountain "beyond the wilderness." He receives the Ten Commandments alone on another mountaintop (Exod 3:1-9; 19:20). Elijah is saved from despair and recalled to God's service under a broom tree "a day's journey into the wilderness"; he subsequently hears God in the silence after earthquake and fire shake a mountain where he stands (1 Kgs 19:4-9, 11-15). Jesus himself repeatedly seeks silence, insight, and God's guidance in the natural world. "In the morning, while it was still very dark," Mark tells us in one such account, "he got up and went out to a deserted place, and there he prayed" (1:35).

Anyone who feels overwhelmed with responsibilities and longs for solitary respite is likely to appreciate the larger context of the latter episode. In the verses immediately preceding the passage just cited, Mark notes that Jesus had spent the previous evening in a very public way ("the whole city was gathered around the door"). The Savior had been completely engaged with the assembly, casting out "many demons" from "all who were sick or possessed" (Mark 1:32-34). He's allowed only a short interval of prayer in the morning, however, before he's pulled back into the fray by disciples who go out to seek him with words reminiscent of guilt-inducing twenty-first-century emails ("When they found him, they said to him, 'Everyone is searching for you,'" Mark 1:36-37).

Even Jesus couldn't escape for very long, the Bible reveals; neither could Moses or Elijah. Immersed in a culture of constant engagement, we twenty-first-century people have very little chance of living in reverent peace for any significant amount of time.

That doesn't mean, however, that we should surrender all hope of ever experiencing wordless sacred serenity. Indeed, the experience might just feel even more wondrous, even more precious because it takes place in the midst of so much clamor.

꙰ ꙰ ꙰

By the time I regain the trailhead dusk is falling. The snowshoe hike has been sublimely uneventful: no mountain lions, no slides or falls, no other human traffic.

And no great spiritual revelations. A heavenly voice has not spoken from an icy sagebrush that suddenly burst into flame; Scout Mountain has not quaked at Jehovah's command.

Still I feel renewed, even transformed. For a few hours, at least, God has drawn me to rest in him.

Week 3

Leaning into Community

9

Participating in Works of Mercy

Delivering Angel Tree Gifts

While the performance of corporal and spiritual acts of mercy is an ongoing responsibility for Catholics, that discipline is especially emphasized in Advent. In our parish, December's weekly bulletins attempt to facilitate compliance with a helpful list of the general behaviors advised: feed the hungry, visit prisoners, admonish sinners, bear wrongs patiently, and so on. Though highly laudable, the items on this roster have always struck me as overwhelming in their aggregate—who could do all those things during one Advent? I suspect that I'm not the only one who has resorted to a so-called "Chinese menu" strategy by checking off at least a few mercies in each column: two hours sorting donations at the food bank, a check written to the homeless shelter, a prayer of forgiveness for a past wrong done to me.

That child's bean-counting perspective was the way I approached the season's call to charity for more than a decade after converting. During the third Advent after my husband's death, however, what began as a mere one-off target of opportunity to "comfort the afflicted" forever deepened and complicated the way I think about mercy.

⚬ ⚬ ⚬

By that December of 2004, the Angel Tree program had long been a regular fixture of our parish's Advent. Its aim was to provide gifts for local children whose parents were spending the holidays in Idaho state prisons. The saintly organizers ascertained from the parents what their children needed or wanted for Christmas and recruited volunteers to buy the gifts, which were delivered in the parents' names. So appealing did altruistic people find this idea that one had to move quickly after mass on the first Sunday in Advent to the little tree hung with requests, or none would remain.

How satisfying it was to search the stores for the gift specified, wrap the package beautifully, and write the gift tag with another's name! How sweet to imagine both parent and child being comforted! And how expeditious a means of heeding Advent's call to charity.

I was among those who never missed a chance to rush to that tree—not until I had to be out of town on Angel Tree Sunday, 2004, that is. A call to the parish office two days later confirmed the foregone conclusion: all gifts were spoken for. "But Susan," Kathy the secretary said, "we were just talking about asking you to help in another way." One of the regular volunteers had recently undergone a knee replacement. Could I possibly donate an afternoon and gasoline on the third Sunday afternoon in December to deliver gifts to some of the children?

The request gave me serious pause. These were families that by definition included criminals. I'd be alone. If a blizzard blew in, even driving around all afternoon would be dangerous.

But I was feeling lonely, invisible, and singled out for misery that December. Few among my acquaintance guessed such a state of mind, for I'd assumed a proud, collected front. On the outside I was proclaiming, "I've got things under control. Your pity is wasted on me." On the inside, I was still trying to imagine a reason why I might want to go on living.

And so I convinced myself that anyone caring for a temporarily orphaned child had to be okay and recalled my new studded snow tires. Longing for comfort and diversion, I remembered the conventional wisdom that doing something nice for others makes the doer feel better.

In retrospect I believe there was also a darker dimension to my acquiescence: the unarticulated sense that encountering others whose circumstances were worse than mine would provide a sort of there-but-for-the-grace-of-God comparative consolation. I'd done something to deserve misery, I imagined back then, or my husband would not have died in his prime. But the people to whom I'd be delivering gifts had obviously done worse things.

"I'm just the messenger," I imagined myself modestly deferring as I reprised the role of a woman living such an emotionally secure and full existence that she could afford to be benevolent—a role no longer mine in reality. "This comes from the little girl's mother. We're only helping out."

Was I ever wrong about the nature of that experience! Before an hour had elapsed on delivery Sunday I felt like one of those well-meaning but clueless middle-class girls in Victorian novels who blithely go out to extend charity to the Other, only to discover that the Other has ideas of his or her own.

The first address indicated a mobile home park often featured in the police log. I stood on a shaky metal front step of a trailer and knocked, more-than-half hoping that nobody was home. "What'd you want?" A shirtless skinny man appeared.

"I have a present for Marilyn from her mother!" I summoned cheerful Lady Bountiful bona fides.

"You know her mother?" The man chuckled (not a pretty sound), snatched the gift, and slammed the door.

The second led to a sprawling apartment complex. No one answered the bell. "Don't worry about it." Kathy's sigh came over my cell phone. "Just bring the gift to the office tomorrow. Sorry about that."

While the first two deliveries confounded warm and fuzzy O. Henry-style fantasies, the following two debunked assumptions about what kind of people went to jail. In the city's toniest neighborhood I stood under a three-story a porte-cochere regarding a vast room, a towering tree, a mountain of gifts. What gall, I thought, for these people to ask others to provide even more presents for their little ones! Pity replaced irritation, however, when I noticed that the older woman (a grandmother?) had retreated to half-hide herself behind the open front door when she understood the nature of my errand.

The road then led to a comfortable middle-class historic neighborhood near the university where I once lived and many of my friends still do. The house was familiar, a craftsman bungalow whose venerable lilacs I'd admired in spring. The woman in the doorway was familiar too, an administrative assistant at the university. Gossip had not presented a whisper of a husband or child in prison, but that had to be the case. Collecting ourselves after a moment of embarrassment, we acted as if the occasion were normal—say, a secret Santa exchange. A little too normal, perhaps.

"Have a Merry Christmas!" I chirped as I turned to go, immediately cursing myself as an idiot.

The final two deliveries were the most revelatory of all. At the penultimate address, three generations shared a too-small space in a manufactured home. A big-screen television blared football; adults and teenagers filled the front room; bowls of popcorn, cans of beer and soda pop heaped the coffee table.

"Oh, for the BABY!" the matriarch finally understood through the din. "Hey, Dakota!!" she shouted. Out of a bedroom walked a beautiful two-year-old girl. Plump and dimpled, she wore a fluffy pink dress. What an incongruous figure she made among folks dressed in low-rider jeans, oversized sweatshirts, and ball caps!

Everybody turned to the child and smiled. "The nice lady brought you a present!" the woman announced. No, I explained, finally getting to use the line I'd practiced. The gift was from the little girl's mother. I was just delivering it.

Nevertheless I was motioned to a chair and the child was lifted to my lap. "Open it now, Dakota!" someone said.

"This is from your mommy," I told her. She beamed and ripped into the paper, revealing a soft baby doll.

"Baby! My baby!" She wrapped the toy in a tight embrace, and mine were not the only eyes in the room that misted.

"Sure you don't want to sit a while and have a beer?" Of course I didn't. Climbing back into the car, however, I almost wished that I'd agreed. Despite the trauma of an incarcerated family member, these people had kept their good humor better than I had. They might have taught me something about bearing hardship.

The last delivery led north beyond the city limits into rural emptiness, out onto the Indian reservation at the edge of the Arco Desert. Dusk loomed as I drove gravel roads, searching for a house in a district where none bore numbers. I backtracked to a known point and read the directions more carefully: drive a mile to the tall stand of pines, turn right onto the unmarked lane, turn left just before the bridge over the first the irrigation canal. . . .

The place was decrepit, just a few rooms enclosed in metal siding under ancient cottonwoods. A knock on the door inspired ferocious barking. Someone inside, though, was shouting for the dogs to calm down, and the slam of an interior door suggested they'd been restrained. My protector was a lanky teenaged boy who nodded with quiet dignity. Once again a child was called—"Ben!"—and an adorable figure emerged from behind the sofa, a black-eyed five-year-old grinning shyly.

His reserve evaporated at the sight of two packages, one each from his father and mother. Ripping them open, he placed the teddy bear in the toy truck and "drove" across the floor, up onto the woodstove, across the back of a dog who hadn't been 86'ed—one who tolerated the proceedings with sleepy good nature though he kept a wary eye on me.

Ben's older brother and I watched, exchanging grins. "Thank you," he said, turning to shake my hand. "He really likes them."

Why hadn't a gift been included for the older brother? Angel Tree perhaps set an age cut-off—I don't know. What I did intuit was that Older Brother and Ben lived alone on the edge of cold waste ground. Though one would assume that a minor would not be allowed to head a household, out on the reservation such things happen. Yet the house was clean and neat and the air smelled of a stew cooking for dinner. The little boy radiated health, security, love.

~⋄~ ~⋄~ ~⋄~

The prayer for those two boys—and for the others—began as I drove home that night, heading south twenty miles through and beyond the city to the place where I now also headed a household on the edge of empty ground. The dense grid of lights that was the city burst into view, infinitely poignant, as the expressway crested a high bench land. Virtually all of those points, I imagined that night, had at one time or another marked a heart in pain.

I'd known in the abstract, of course, that suffering could intrude on wealth and education as well as on poverty, on happy families as well as on troubled ones. I understood that loss would leave its mark on the angry, the overwhelmed, the brave and clueless alike. But the experience of delivering Angel Tree gifts made the understanding concrete.

That was the Advent—the day—when the generality of human misery first came home to me, jolting me out of the impression that no one knew suffering like mine. My heart opened, unbidden, breaking the dam of singled-out resentment and clearing the way for others' mercy to start seeping in. "Why me?" I realized that December afternoon in 2004, is a question that only an oblivious fool would ask.

As that general and (to me) revelatory charity of heart lingered and informed the season that followed, small unrehearsed works of mercy flowed from my hand as if of their own accord. A person who acknowledges her membership in a community of afflicted human brothers and sisters, I discovered, doesn't need a checklist.

Our parish hasn't participated in Angel Tree for some years now. The effects linger in my case, however (as I hope they do for at least some of those children and parents), since each Advent refreshes the lessons of that delivery Sunday. Each December when I catch myself conceptualizing mercy merely as something to be extended from a position of strength, I commit to replacing the calcification that has crept into my heart of stone with beating, empathetic flesh. I look into other faces, other hearts, and let myself respond to what I find there. I acknowledge that I too need human as well as divine mercy. I attempt to open to receiving both graciously.

And when Christmas finally comes, I hear the haunting apocalyptic third verse of an old favorite Christmas carol with new ears:

> And ye, beneath life's crushing load,
> Whose forms are bending low,
> Who toil along the climbing way
> With painful steps and slow,
> Look now! For glad and golden hours
> Come swiftly on the wing.
> O rest beside the weary road,
> And hear the angels sing!

10

Loving One Another

Choosing Presents for Friends and Family

Gifts—for family, friends, acquaintances, and even strangers as in the case of programs like Angel Tree—are such a staple of contemporary Christmas that some might be unaware that giving them is a relatively recent addition to the season. In truth, the modern custom of exchanging holiday presents became popular only in the second half of the nineteenth century. Many Christmas trappings that we take for granted can be traced in the English-speaking world to that Victorian era, including Christmas trees, Santa Claus, Christmas cards, and classic carols.

In a theological sense, of course, the concept of "gift" has always been central to the Advent and Christmas stories. "For God so loved the world that he gave his only Son, so that everyone who believes in him may not perish but may have eternal life," John writes in the quintessential verse (3:16). Jesus' coming represents the ultimate gift; he literally embodies grace. Purely from his own goodness God has offered us salvation and eternal life, the very gifts for which we most long for as our mortal days tick by.

The wise men's offerings to the baby Jesus presage our modern custom of giving material things. As every Christian knows, the Magi are said to have traveled a great distance to the manger after divining that a marvelous king would be born. Following the star of Bethlehem, they brought three gifts: frankincense (used in Jewish ceremonies) to suggest that Christ would be worshipped; gold to indicate his kingly status; and myrrh (employed in preparing bodies for burial) to presage his suffering and death on the cross. In these absolutely appropriate gifts, they showed deep and accurate knowledge of the baby's essence.

Would that all the gifts we give each other in the twenty-first century could be so apt and the process of giving so dignified. Too often today the process of choosing presents for others becomes a significant source of Christmas stress instead of a celebration of connection. There's even a formal term for the state into which we work ourselves at the very thought of exchanging presents: "holiday gift anxiety." The blast of seasonal advertisements that begins before Thanksgiving raises our expectations about giving (and receiving) to unrealistic levels. We worry about reciprocity: is this gift enough in light of what the recipient gave me last year? We fret over whether the person who receives the offering will like it. We're embarrassed when someone for whom we've not bought a gift gives us one. If we are honest, most of us will admit that on occasion we've been disappointed when we opened what others proffered.

The very etymology of the word "present" as applied to gifts suggests that such anxiety is not a new phenomenon, although media pressures have undoubtedly raised the stakes. Among the word's sources are the Old French and Medieval Latin verbs *presenter* and *praesentare*, which signified formally placing an offering before someone. A variant meaning of those verbs indicates "to offer for inspection," connoting that insecurity and anticipation of judgment are built into the very concept of a gift.

While such anxiety is perhaps inevitable when one offers tribute to a feudal lord (or a modern boss), it's an unfortunate emotion to feel when trading gifts with people for whom we profess to feel affection. How sad it is to mire ourselves in insecurity and competition in the very course of celebrating the ultimate divine free-will offering!

~&~ ~&~ ~&~

Gift-giving and anxiety don't necessarily have to go hand-in-hand, however, as a woman I once knew, now gone to her reward, demonstrated. Amy's strategy was inspired. She used the process of choosing a present as an opportunity to pay deeper attention to those she loved. Not for Amy the reasonable advice of directly asking people what they wanted. Instead she observed and listened through the year to intuit what people needed or longed for, extending Advent's spirit of loving fellowship into a perpetual habit of mind.

Her gifts reflected a breathtaking degree of attention. Unwrapping a large hand-thrown ceramic colander one December, I recalled that she'd kept me company in the kitchen as I put the finishing touches on an August dinner party. That afternoon draining the pasta took forever because my wire strainer was too small. I received earrings I'd admired at a craft fair we attended together (she'd snuck back later that day and bought them for me). Knowing that spring yard clean-up would be especially arduous for me the year after Ford died (I'd had no energy to do any clearing the previous autumn) she provided a gift certificate for a day of work by a lawn service.

The effect of receiving such a gift was that of having "been fully known," to borrow a phrase from 1 Corinthians' beautiful chapter on love. "Love is patient; love is kind; love is not envious or boastful or rude," the verses read, celebrating everlasting, selfless love as greater even than faith or hope (13:4). Amy modeled all of those characteristics. She stayed patient with her friends, seeking not to impose or impress but to understand. Seldom expensive in monetary terms, the objects she gave became priceless reminders of essential human connection, souvenirs of the greater gifts of attentiveness and loving intimacy.

~◇~ ~◇~ ~◇~

One of the great features of Amy's strategy, as I've discovered on adopting it, is the way it deepens a sense of connection for the giver as well as for the receiver. In order to discern what gifts a friend should receive one must listen and observe with perhaps more care than one might otherwise have invested. One learns new things about and discovers new nuances in even the most familiar others. The process is thoroughly fascinating, a wonderful corrective to the tendency to take for granted the people with whom one lives in marriage, family, and community.

There's also a pragmatic seasonal bonus. Paying attention in this way makes Advent a lot easier, since by December a skillful noticer has probably already conceived of, if not yet bought, gifts for just about everybody.

This year the designated gift shelf in my bedroom closet holds an array à la Amy. A turquoise bracelet rests there, destined for a best friend with whom I once shared a glorious visit to Santa Fe. She'll recognize the Native American market style and understand that I was thinking of her while attending a meeting in that city this past October. A newly published book on cranes waits for a companion who glows with joy whenever she sees or hears a sandhill crane on spring mountain hikes. Another who has said that she'd like to learn "fancy cooking" now that she's retired is getting a promise for a day-long cooking lesson in French cuisine from yours truly. One of my goddaughters, obsessed with chocolate cuisine, is receiving a set of chocolate molds from an online specialty catalog she's confessed to reading as recreation. My sister back in Philadelphia, who documents on Facebook her attentive care for a host of stray cats, will unwrap a gift card to Petco.

Handmade items with an I-know-you component are among the assembly, massed in their own separate crate. A knitted infinity scarf will soon join my church singing partner Beth's wardrobe (the duplicate of one she admired on me, but in her favorite purple). To my chagrin, however, that's the only completed object that the crate currently holds. I'm in the midst of knitting H a pair of fingerless gloves that he can use while fly fishing in the spring and autumn chill; he recently waxed nostalgic for a pair he'd lost years ago. I'm about two evenings away from finishing a hat made in washable wool for a nurse who flies with the local emergency helicopter crew. Farther out—indeed, now appearing as balls of yarn only—are three hats for new babies. *They'll be quick*, I tell myself resolutely as the third week of Advent speeds by. *But it's time to get serious.*

In the service of such handmade offerings I sit up late as I do every December, knitting. I fend off sleepiness with unfamiliar wee-hours television programs. I work through the Netflix queue and binge-watch television series on Amazon Instant Video: *Mad Men, Downton Abbey, Call the Midwife*. Sometimes music provides company, including this year's Advent playlist, the Benjamin Britten *St. Nicholas Cantata* or *Ceremony of Carols*, the *Messiah*, the Celtic Christmas series. The latter is especially dear because I wouldn't know it except for Ford, who gave me a yearly Christmas CD.

Watching the constellations wheel slowly above a mountain ridge, I think of the person for whom the evening's garment is destined. I relive good times together (or in the case of the babies, imagine their good times to come). I remember recipients' troubles. I picture the person wearing the piece and imagine how the very stitches I'm shaping at that moment will warm and adorn.

"Prayer shawls"—the fiber artists' term for comforting wraps created for the ill, dying, caregivers, and bereaved—aren't the only homemade garments with prayers woven into them.

⊱ ⊱ ⊱

Though the medieval roots of the word "present" can be a little discouraging to all who dream of open-hearted, unconditionally happy seasonal gift exchanges, an interesting thing happens when one simply says the word. In my dialect, at least, when the word is varied to a plural noun ("presents") it becomes a homonym for a word with a quite different affect: "presence." Amy would certainly approve of that congruence. And that echo is not in fact just wishful thinking or the accident of pronunciation. Deep in the long list of root words for "present," way back beyond the feudal-sounding associations, is the Latin term "inpraesent," which means "face-to-face."

This connotation holds special implications for Christians, who celebrate a miraculous kind of face-to-face encounter during the high season of gift exchanges. As Matthew reminds us, we wait during Advent for someone called "Emmanuel," a name that means "God is with us" (1:23). By sending his son, God registers his ever-present concern for us. Just as happens with our spouses, children, and friends, we may slip into taking this eminently loving

God for granted. But he never stints in omnipresent, loving attention to us.

That's a good thing to remember on a cold December night. Engaged in the work of human hands, physically alone but wrapped in loving thoughts of others, I turn to a God who sees our secret desires, who honors us continually with his presence.

"Hold those who will wear these garments in your heart, Lord," I pray, aloud and with words this time. "Hold me there, too."

11

Facing Mutability

Trimming the Tree

There's nothing like a lifetime of Christmases to drive home a hard truth: in our mortal form we're creatures whose element is mutability. As people enter or leave our holiday celebrations, as our material circumstances or health change and our faith deepens or falters, as our worries and our dreams evolve, the nature of our observance of Christ's birth changes. Comparisons to Christmases past are inevitable. "Remember when we trimmed the tree in the old house?" we ask each other. "Remember how cold it was when we went caroling that first Christmas when the kids were little?" "Remember Mom's Christmas dinners?" The very rituals we build to reassure ourselves of continuity remind us that the circumstances of our lives inevitably evolve.

"All is vanity," Ecclesiastes pronounces in a somber expression of the latter truth, citing the passing of generations and the impermanence of human efforts and pleasures. Urging his hearers to enjoy their days while they can, the speaker nevertheless insists that all earthly pleasures will fade.

Even the biblical texts that announce Christ's birth remind the faithful of mutability. While inspiring joy at the nativity, they also contain dark reminders of the turns that the Savior's circumstances will take toward the end of his earthly sojourn. There's that myrhh, and more directly Jesus' own foretelling three times of his death and resurrection (Mark 8:31-32; 9:30-31; 10:33-34). Advent readings also include post-resurrection texts like the story of doubting Thomas (John 20:24-29).

"Sorrowing, sighing, bleeding, dying / Sealed in a stone-cold tomb"—a middle verse of "We Three Kings" is explicit about what lays in store for that baby in the manger. This particular passage disquieted me so much when I was a child that I could hardly sing it. Why *couldn't* we be allowed to revel innocently in December's happiness for at least a little while?

As I've aged and suffered my own losses, however, such reminders of mortality during the holidays have come to seem very wise, even essential. They're realistic. Even though we may know complete happiness at a particular time, our lives will include sorrow and death. Knowing that even Christ, the Son of God, suffered and died before rising again, we're encouraged to imagine our own difficulties as part of a larger, ultimately triumphant pattern.

"Look to him in your fear," wrote the great theologian Dietrich Bonhoeffer (who died in a Nazi concentration camp), calling Jesus "the One who alone conquered fear" by assuring our salvation. Those who align themselves with Christ, Bonhoeffer says, "know a hope, and that hope is: Thy will be done."

~ ~ ~

I take the tiny blown-glass hummingbird from its padded box, remembering the August afternoon when my husband and I bought it in an artist's studio, not much more than a room with big windows overlooking the rocky Maine coast. This ornament was such a natural souvenir, one that would bridge the happiness of that vacation week and the home happiness we knew back in Idaho. Even as we watched it being wrapped and put into this box for the first time, we were already thinking with pleasure of the hummingbirds buzzing in that season in our own backyard three thousand miles away, creatures we'd soon see again. "Rainbows with bodies," Ford had called hummingbirds in one of his poems, and he'd repeated the phrase as light from the studio window caught this ornament. That Christmas the purchase brought the happy spirit of that August day and the sound of the sea into the room. It almost seemed an affirmation or a charm to insure that living hummingbirds would return in the proper season to our frozen mountainside.

The first Christmas after Ford died I discovered that I could not place that ornament on the tree—indeed, I could not bear even to open its box or handle it. The same was true for so many other cherished objects in the Christmas storage box. The sweet creche animals Ford gave me on our first Christmas together, the art-glass sphere we chose together in Seattle to commemorate our tenth anniversary (holding our breath at its cost), the little framed pictures of us together on mountain summits. Even—or especially—the silly objects that diffused too-high seriousness. Just a glimpse of our standard tree-topper (a goofy-looking parrot I'd glued together out of bright felt and Styrofoam as part of a pirate Halloween costume for Ford) made me dizzy and physically ill.

To allow that first tree of the new disposition to stand bereft of all bright decoration would have been too vivid a symbol, however. It ended up adorned with the only two kinds of objects in the box that I could handle: the Metropolitan Museum of Art yearly issue Christmas stars I'd begun acquiring before our marriage and the sand dollars we'd picked up on "our" beach in Washington State. The latter had always been tucked into greens on the sideboard, never previously hung on the tree, but enhanced with hangers hot-glued onto the backs they seemed to belong there. So did all-white lights instead of the usual colored ones.

The irony, not lost on me then or now, was that Ford would have preferred this style of decoration to the heavily trimmed trees of our past. "Crud-encrusted," he'd teasingly called them. Guilty tears came that first year even as I surveyed the results. *Why couldn't you have given him the pleasure of having a tree in his taste while he was alive?* The slippery slope gaped with horrible implications: *You always let him down.*

Surely sadness, even despair, is a common response to trimming a first Christmas tree after loss. How could one not feel a surreal aversion on performing this once-joyful ritual in a world transformed? The person is gone but the objects remain, mocking reminders that the future once glowed with promise.

The process must be exponentially difficult for those who have lost a child—all those school-picture ornaments and darling objects made in school or scouts, or constructed at the kitchen table with the very parent who shudders on uncovering them. After divorces undesired by the one trimming the tree, the memories must also be devastating (though I imagine that there might be some smashing in such cases). And for survivors of suicides . . . .

~◦~ ~◦~ ~◦~

It did not occur to me during that first Christmas as a widow—nor the next, nor the next—to buy any new ornaments of my own, for I had adopted a sort of end-time mentality. Living without my husband felt unbearable, so I comforted myself with the assurance that I'd soon be following him. Fighting down religious anomie (and closing my ears to the seductive song of the black hole such nihilism inspired), I managed to constructed a mental scenario that explained my temporarily continued presence on earth: God must be keeping me around until I'd done some particular thing he intended. Does this sound insane? Perhaps, but it was what I taught myself to believe as a new widow.

In consequence I felt a rush of glee on every occasion when I managed to accomplish something useful (and such things happened, proving that God can employ people in just about any state). Perhaps taking a particular struggling student under my wing was The Thing. An exhausted single mother, she'd been about to drop out of college. Yet she had so much potential as a writer. With patience and encouragement, advice and tutoring, I'd helped to convince her to carry on. I imagined the people her talent would touch over the next fifty years, offering them up to God, and waited in happy anticipation for my personal rapture.

Or perhaps it was training a group of teaching assistants, passing on the legacy of three decades in the classroom (ditto for touching their future students). Various pieces of writing and the oral history project I directed at St. Gertrude's seemed likely candidates. When I wrote a book of meditations for teachers based on saints' lives and it became a modest bestseller, I was certain that the account had been balanced.

Not a whisper came from the heavens at any of these achievements, however. After a while I noticed a persistent pattern. As soon as one task was ending, another irresistible call arose. I began to suspect that God was seducing me back to a longterm commitment to this world.

It is a measure of how deranged I was that at first this notion depressed me. I wanted to be with Ford, not languishing on earth as a "remnant" of my husband (to use a term from eras past). Gradually, however, it became clear that I did not have a choice. Grudging acceptance followed.

Much more time passed, however, until I abandoned a particular nutty recurring behavior of early widowhood, though I did perform it with an increasing measure of self-conscious irony. After some new potential Thing had been accomplished, I'd take myself ceremoniously out onto the deck after dark, stand dead center, and look up at the stars. "Is that sufficient?" I'd demand aloud, spreading my hands wide in a gesture of supplication. "Can you beam me up now?"

Obviously such miraculous translation did not happen. The tasks have multiplied and diverged over nearly a decade and a half, and I've stopped anticipating The Thing. Only God knows what twists and turns of work and mutability remain ahead. I've made peace with the fact that the only possible appropriate response to life's vicissitudes for a person of faith is to ride them with confidence in the mystery that shapes them. "In the morning sow your seed, and at evening do not let your hands be idle; for you do not know which will prosper, this or that, or whether both alike will be good," writes Ecclesiastes. "Send out your bread upon the waters, for after many days you will get it back" (11:1, 6).

❧ ❧ ❧

The decorations on my Christmas trees have multiplied with the "many days" and the moderation of grief, though mine remains a relatively restrained display. The little animals and birds have crept back. The art glass ornament, the hummingbird, and Ford's mother's little straw angels have retaken their places among the branches. I've even purchased some new adornments, including gold and silver balls, and little birds' nests with eggs inside. I've changed the kind of trees I buy, acquiescing that the thick Scotch pines and grand firs we favored during our marriage are too much for me to handle alone. Now I trim alpine firs, ponderosa pines, and similar airy specimens with small-diameter trunks and lacy foliage. At first such varieties seemed too sparse, but I've grown to love the way they allow space between their branches.

This year's model is a sturdy but slender local Douglas fir that stretches almost to the ceiling. I choose a high but substantial branch, far from the potential batting of my three cats and bumping of guests during the big Christmas party, and attach the glass hummingbird, twisting its wire tightly, placing this particular rainbow far enough out from the trunk that it will catch the light. Then I step back to check the effect and like what I see: a tree sparkling its joy through the window glass into the darkness beyond.

For a moment I catch myself thinking of this tree as yet another "Thing." Even as I smile at this discarded habit of mind, it strikes me that there's some truth in that perception.

Putting up this tree is surely not my ultimate Thing, not by a long shot. It is, however, an action whose consequences may serve God. In a few days the display I've just constructed will stand as an affirmation to the people gathered here, churched and unchurched alike, for a party celebrating Christ's birth.

I hope that at least some of them see this tree as more than a seasonal totem. In my eyes, at least, it seems on this night nothing less than a proclamation. Despite the fact of human mutability, it demonstrates that renewal is possible. In the face of loss, with God's help the woman who lives here has kept faith. Acceding to "Thy will be done" can be a very difficult process indeed—but it can ultimately bring renewal.

12

Acknowledging Generosity

Cooking with Children

The two little girls peeped as joyfully as springtime birds all through that December afternoon in 1993. That day we made Christmas cutout sugar cookies using my grandmother's recipe and the collection of cookie cutters I'd inherited. Elizabeth (Pamela and Russell's daughter, to whom I am surrogate godmother) shared the songs she'd recently learned in kindergarten. She waxed especially enthusiastic about a tune whose title she announced as "Reindeer Paws" (a.k.a. "Up on the housetop, reindeer pause"). Kate, a year younger and always eager to do whatever Elizabeth did, chimed in with happy bellowing.

Their mothers had confessed at a gathering the previous weekend that they'd fallen hopelessly behind in Christmas preparation. What they needed was a childless interval to shop, wrap, decorate—or just to take a nap. So I invited the two girls to join me.

Ford and I married when he was forty-four and I was thirty-five; we had no children. Though we assured each other that our students, the products of our writing desks, and each other were family enough, I was in my forties by the year Elizabeth and Kate joined me in the kitchen and feeling the absence of little ones with a sadness that took me by surprise. Making my grandmother's cookies alone for the past few years had felt, honestly, a bit hollow. I'd caught myself dwelling morbidly on the fact that there was no one to whom I could pass along any of my Christmas traditions, including this one.

In advance I'd imagined our little cookie party in sentimental Norman Rockwell focus. In that picture the two little girls stood on stools to reach the counter, entranced by the embellishments: red and green sugar, spicy-smelling cinnamon hearts, chocolate sprinkles, and tiny multicolored balls, glowing dragées like the ones my brother and I always understood that we weren't supposed to eat (advice we ignored, as I suspect all children do). I anticipated that the girls would be adorable in their serious focus, that they'd enjoy hearing Christmas carols playing softly in the background.

The Advent baking party in 1993 was nothing like that. Giddy with excitement and relaxed (they'd known me from babyhood), Elizabeth and Kate grabbed cookie cutters and attacked the rolled-out dough surface. The shapes tore as the girls tried to lift them from the counter; the delicate dough grew progressively more sticky. The girls' voices drowned out the CD player and I turned it off. Our "background" music consisted of enthusiastic staples of the elementary school canon (the aforementioned "Reindeer Paws," "All I Want for Christmas Is My Two Front Teeth," "Santa Claus is Coming to Town") and everything-old-is-new-again daring alternative phrasings of traditional carols ("It was loaded, it exploded!!!"). Egg wash spilled; colored sugar and chocolate sprinkles flew in all directions; silver dragees and cinnamon hearts rolled across the wooden floor. After territorial

outbursts ("Hey! That's MY cookie! You're gettin' it on MINE!")
I separated the cutouts onto "hers" and "hers" baking sheets. Managing time proved difficult. Kate focused intently, taking many minutes to channel just the right sugar color for each shape and arrange the Christmas tree "balls" and lines of "lights" just so, while Elizabeth essentially threw decorations at her creations—a purple camel, an angel with one blue and one silver eye.

At the end of an hour we'd accomplished twenty cookies—six museum pieces and fourteen exuberantly bizarre creations. Three additional balls of dough remained to be rolled out, but the girls had had enough and were ready to splash in the outdoor hot tub. As I delivered them home, damp-haired and sleepy-eyed ninety minutes later, each stood very tall as she handed her plate of cookies to her mother. There was much exclamation. "Can we do this again next year?" Kate asked.

"I'm not sure you ever lasted even an hour." My mother's what-did-you-expect intonation came loud and clear through 3,000 miles of telephone line. "And what a commotion you and Johnny always made!"

Nevertheless I persisted with the custom again the next year, just as my mother had. Other children joined Elizabeth and Kate; other foods appeared on the agenda after participants expressed interest in learning to make them. I taught little ones, then tweens, then even a few young teenagers to make those sugar cookies, along with gingerbread people, yeast pretzels, cinnamon swirl bread, chocolate truffles, and Christmas-themed pizza.

In retrospect it seems incredible that those parents would have shared their precious children with me, blithely dropping the young ones off for an afternoon in the care of a woman who claimed precisely *zero* childrearing experience. But they did.

More extensive yet was the confidence extended by parents of the dozen girls who enrolled in the Girl Scout troop I organized for Elizabeth when she entered first grade. Despite a fingers-crossed approach at the start, the project blossomed. For eight years the girls, my coleader, and I shared songs and crafts, hikes and camping, service projects at the zoo and the homeless daycare center, science inquiry, and cooking. We taught them to cross-country and downhill ski, to quilt, and to recognize the constellations. They explored careers by shadowing women we'd enlisted. On a weeklong troop road trip to Washington State's Olympic Peninsula several saw the ocean for the first time. We listened to their troubles, celebrated their triumphs, and watched them grow. "My girls," I still call them.

Things changed as they entered junior high school. The girls grew absorbed in extracurricular activities. Girl Scouts obviously seemed to them like a remnant of their childhood (though being sweet girls they played along for one more year), and we finally dissolved the troop by mutual consent. I mourned but had other things on my mind at that juncture. Ford had recently been diagnosed with cancer. Their loss became the first of the progressive losses that began my twenty-first century, a void soon absorbed into a greater void. You might say that I became simultaneously the first empty nester in our circle as well as the first widow.

~◦~ ~◦~ ~◦~

One girl among them, however, proved faithful through adolescence and has been cooking with me for two decades at this writing. Unlike cherished others I could mention, Lara proved so disciplined, so eager to learn, and so naturally talented in the kitchen that when she turned ten I undertook what seemed at the time like an iffy experiment, inviting her to help make hors d'oeuvres for the annual Christmas party.

That first December Lara had never seen many of the herbs, cheeses, specialized pans and tools on my counter, but she seemed to know instinctively what to do with them. Enveloped in an oversized apron, she filled tartlets and topped bruschetta, evincing flair as well as attention. At the afternoon's end I invited her back for the next December.

Thus began our enduring tradition. In the second iteration I assigned Lara a simple recipe to prepare start-to-finish. "I MADE that!" she proclaimed when her mother arrived to pick her up, gesturing with pride. Her responsibilities and expertise grew; before many winters passed I was vetting inspired brainstorms ("What would you think if I put some curry in this turnover?" "Would it be ok to use a little grated orange peel in this chocolate?"). When I admired Lara's knife skills, she admitted that she'd been watching Julia Child.

So soon, it seemed, Lara was driving herself to my house on those pre-party December afternoons. Thanks to her new independent mobility we added a planning meeting to the calendar, a session at a coffee shop on the Friday before Thanksgiving. At first I was the one who provided all the recipes, but in Lara's last year of high school I loosened the reins. "Surprise me," I told her. "Find a dish or two that would complement what we have—something you're interested in trying from a cookbook or a magazine. Then just give me a shopping list. Your choice!" The hors d'oeuvres she added to the roster joined the party's greatest hits.

Though I'd long feared that what I knew about cooking and hostessing would die with me (along with so much else), I discovered that I'd acquired an heir.

⚬ ⚬ ⚬

Cooking with children seemed such a simple thing at the start—fun, messy, incidental. Over time, though, I came to understand it as a breathtaking gift.

There was that generosity on the parents' part, for one thing—generosity whose implications deepened as I became not just a shortterm babysitter but a frequent custodian of their children. As any Girl Scout leader who takes the job seriously knows, the position entails acting as a model of adult behavior and a transmitter of values. Such was the case for me. I became through long acquaintance a sort of extra parent or favorite aunt, someone whose words were repeated at family dinner tables ("SUSAN says," parents would imitate cheerfully in their daughters' intonations when we met). What we did together shaped lifelong hobbies, reading, beliefs, careers (one of those girls actually works for the Girl Scout council in a neighboring state). In the cases of Elizabeth and Lara I was accepted as almost a sort of comother, folded into families with an easy, generous hospitality that I'm pretty sure I'd have had trouble extending to an outsider.

My childless state had seemed inevitable. Suddenly I *was* mentoring children, and to my surprise able and happy to do it. Life transformed as it opened to the pleasures, the challenges, and the anxieties of a connection with young people that didn't end after a semester or two. The world became infinitely more complex, infinitely richer.

⚬ ⚬ ⚬

As a Catholic I dare to believe that God's grace as well as human generosity made that opening possible. This claim is not meant in any way to suggest that I think myself exceptional; in our faith we hold that the hand of the divine reaches not just to extraordinary people (prophets and saints and such) but to everyone. The *Catechism of the Catholic Church* affirms that God actively shapes our nature, giving us both the desire to seek and serve him and the means to do so. It's an article of our faith that we receive the capacity to do what he has in mind, "the gifts that the Spirit grants us to associate us with his work" (2003).

Mentoring little girls was certainly not a sort of "work" I imagined for myself at age forty, back when I was making a life as a scholar, professor, and member of a self-contained, newly married couple too old to start a family. I'd always been convinced that I wouldn't have made much of a mother—too impatient, too insecure, too self-absorbed. The call seemingly came out of nowhere; the tools sprang to use before I even realized I held them in my hands. But they were good tools, judging by how the girls have turned out. They're ethical, kind, intellectually curious, accomplished, and loving. Many are engaged in helping professions; none has gone astray. Their parents, of course, had the most to do with this trajectory, but the association with me apparently did not hurt.

&ropsilon; &ropsilon; &ropsilon;

When Lara went off to college in Montana I assumed that our Christmas party cooking sessions would end. She, however, held no such assumption. During her undergraduate work we chose the party date so that she'd be able to drive home after finals in time for a day of cooking. Even when she studied abroad—in Europe, in South America—she somehow managed to appear in my kitchen on the third weekend in December. She's graduated and is married now, working as an engineer two hundred miles away.

Nevertheless we consult on menus over the Internet, and each year she drives down the continent's western spine after work on the third Friday in December, bursting through the door at noon on Saturday morning with a fresh apron and a familiar smile.

We're friends rather than mentor-and-student now, and thanks to long practice in each other's company we've become more efficient. This year we're so far ahead that we feel free to take a break in midafternoon to do Internet research for a summer trip we hope to take together to a distant city where we'll run a half marathon. Half an hour before the guests arrive everything is plated and we've changed into fancy dress. Lighting the candles, we pour a sample of champagne, surveying the millions of glorious calories waiting to be consumed. "To next year," Lara says, raising her glass.

The doorbell rings. Her family enters, and I smile as she moves to her young husband's side. H arrives, puts his arm around me, and insists on taking photos of Lara and me with the bounty before it disappears.

Soon the room is so full I can't see the door. People, as usual, just let themselves in; they all know to pile their coats back on the bed. Talk and laughter crest. I'm turning from one conversation toward another when a tap comes on my shoulder. *Elizabeth*, to my surprise, is home from her second year at the University of Washington medical school three days earlier than expected for my party. "Remember when we made these?" she asks, brandishing a butter cookie coated in blue sugar in the shape of an angel. Then she hugs me.

What a wonderful web of love enfolds us, using us so inexorably, so marvelously, in its service. What a magnificent God cares for us, wisely and patiently finding a way to reveal to us gifts we've never imagined we might hold!

Week 4

~❧~

Celebrating on the Doorstep

13

Honoring God's Creation

Feeding Birds in the National Forest

On the fourth Sunday afternoon in Advent my custom has long been to venture again out into the national forest. Like the previous expedition in early December this one involves backcountry travel, a break from holiday preparations, and quiet time in nature. Its focus is different, though, echoing the season's progression. The time for taking-stock has passed; the period of patient waiting is nearly over. Advent's later days call us to move outward instead of inward, to anticipate culmination as our preparations segue into the harvest of Christmas joy.

In that spirit of sociability I've always invited a companion on this second outing—just one, since the event falls immediately after the boisterous-enough Christmas party. Nevertheless the day entails its own antic festivity, its own distinctive brand of singing and dancing among the participants, for it involves the literal birds of the air. On that day we go to fill feeders in an aspen grove three miles up a trail where a box canyon ends in a cul-de-sac of steep snow slopes.

I've always thought of the expedition's purpose as offering more than mere nutrition. Perhaps I'm being fanciful, but I always imagine visiting these wildings as an exercise in fellowship, an invitation to join us humans in the celebration of Christ's birth.

⚬ ⚬ ⚬

"Eco-spirituality"—an ethos that affirms the spiritual connection between humans and the environment—is a relatively recent term, but Christianity has long acknowledged humanity's integral connection to the rest of the created world. In the first chapter of Genesis, on the very day after God creates earth's creatures and immediately after God creates humans, he gives the latter "dominion over the fish of the sea and over the fowl of the air and over every living thing that moves upon the earth" (1:24-30).

One interpretation of these words has assumed that the word "dominion" is equivalent to "domination": that God intended to assign humans the duty to subjugate the earth. Some sects (including American Puritans) went so far as to consider untamed nature dangerous, the devil's domain. Some held, and some conservatives still hold, that undue focus on the material world gives too much emphasis to our physical being, distracting us from our souls.

Despite such contentions, many prominent Christian thinkers have asserted that God's created world should be treated with holy respect. Saint Francis of Assisi famously considered all living creatures (as well as the sun and moon and plants) beloved brothers and sisters. He preached, it is reported, not just to sentient creatures but also to flowers. The mendicant order he founded maintains this reverence for nature as a manifestation of God's love.

Though Francis is the best-known historical proponent of respectful connection with the material world, other influential Catholics have shared this point of view. Among them is St. Benedict, who insisted that members of the monastic order he established perform *labora* (work) in the everyday world as well as spend time in *ora* (prayer). Benedictines go out into the fields as well as into the chapel; they are instructed in the Rule of St. Benedict to take thoughtful care of tools and resources. As the members of the Conference of American Benedictine Prioresses put it in their 1980 statement "Of All Good Gifts": "A spirit of reverence for all creation permeates the Rule, together with a sense of oneness with the land, the days, the seasons." Those who follow Benedict, the sisters explain, are "impelled to preserve, cherish, and nurture all that is touched by the Creator's hand."

The group of Benedictines I know best, the sisters of St. Gertrude in Idaho, consider responsible stewardship of the earth so important that they have affirmed it as a mission statement priority. Their community has been "entrusted with the gift of land by our loving God and Creator," they write; they prefer to think of themselves as *responsible for* rather than *owners of* the land in northern Idaho on which their community has lived for a century. "Listening with the ear of our heart to the wisdom expressed through creation opens us to the deeper reality of God in our lives," they affirm.

The notion that religion and environmental awareness are compatible has achieved up-to-the-minute prominence through the words of our current Pope Francis, disseminated in the pages of his 2015 encyclical, On Care for Our Common Home (*Laudato Si*). Acknowledging global warming and calling for reform, the pope terms the earth "a sister [who] now cries out to us because of the harm we have inflicted on her by our irresponsible use and abuse of the goods with which God has endowed her." Francis reminds us that the Bible itself emphasizes the earth's holiness, quoting Wisdom 13:5: "Through the greatness, and the beauty of creatures one comes to know by analogy their maker." "Rather than a problem to be solved, the world is a joyful mystery to be contemplated with gladness and praise," he writes.

∾ ∾ ∾

One of the many biblical episodes in which the natural world plays an integral and interactive background to human doings is the Christmas story. Besides the star and the night landscape in which the shepherds watch, the nativity scene is by implication full of animals. Mary and Joseph take refuge in a stable where the animals accompanying inn visitors would have been domiciled; the infant Christ is laid in a manger. Shepherds imply sheep; the wise men must have ridden mounts of some sort. The very first extant artistic renderings of Jesus' birth (paintings and stonework dating from the fourth century) depict oxen, asses, and camels. Later art almost invariably does also. Crèches complete with living animals (the first credited to St. Francis himself) have inspired devotions since the thirteenth century.

A fanciful folk tradition from medieval times imagined Christmas Eve as a special time for beasts. In honor of the original manger animals' reverent watchfulness, the lore held that all animals can speak at midnight on Christmas Eve. While in modern times we may not actually believe that superstition, children today still echo it whenever they sing "The Friendly Beasts," a carol dating from the late Middle Ages. In that song various animals—"the donkey shaggy and brown," "the cow all white and red," and "the dove, from rafters high"—boast of the services that they were privileged to render to the infant Jesus. "The Friendly Beasts" is not just a museum or nursery piece, either: it was included along with more contemporary expressions of the same theme in Art

Garfunkle's 1986 holiday album *The Animals' Christmas*. The appeal of reverent, speaking animals who celebrate Christ's birth is evidently still so great that the collection became a bestseller.

⚬ ⚬ ⚬

I can't tell you whether the ravens and downy woodpeckers, nuthatches and finches up Kinney Creek do speak at midnight on Christmas Eve—I'm always otherwise engaged, and anyway it's much too cold to hike up to the aspen grove in December darkness. What I can affirm is that they're not shy about expressing appreciation in their own language at more human-friendly times.

Ford was my first partner on the yearly Advent bird feeding trips; after he died I invited a colleague's daughter a little too old for the Girl Scout troop but still happy to be mentored. A member of the local cross-country ski team, even as a young adolescent Camille was undaunted by the expedition's physical demands and sturdy enough to carry a backpack bearing bags of bird seed and suet cakes.

Our mode of transportation has varied with the weather. We've skied in when the snow was fluffy or smoothly packed, and hiked on snowshoes when conditions were less favorable. Once Camille and I picked our gingerly way over patches of treacherous ice wearing hiking boots equipped with strap-on crampons. The expedition's animate scenery has also varied. We've almost always seen deer, occasionally moose, once a sidelong flash of a startled bobcat.

This year Camille is heavily pregnant with the son she and her husband will welcome in February. Even in the best of conditions it would be unthinkable for her to trek up the canyon. And so I travel instead with H. He's a serious environmentalist and Audubon Society member, pretty set in his beliefs. I debated inviting him, imagining the worthy objections to this errand that he might raise: *those birds find plenty to eat at that site already or they wouldn't be there; we don't want to habituate them to a food supply that disappears; inviting them to congregate can draw predators. You're just being sentimental.*

To my relief he's offered none of those canards; indeed, he seems excited about the project. The snow is abundant and perfectly consolidated; we ski companionably together up the long climb from the trailhead. We comment on the animal tracks beside the trail (a moose has walked here recently, though he or she is not currently in evidence) and on the mares-tail clouds that indicate a coming storm. H identifies a sharp-shinned hawk as the source of a cry that echoes overhead.

My heart warms as we reach the aspen grove and see that someone else has brought suet cakes to fill the wire cage feeders I always leave in place. There's no sense in taking ours back down the hill, so H (always meticulously prepared in the out-of-doors, as was Ford), takes rope from his pack and threads it through the holes he pokes in our suet cakes. He hangs them on the branches; we fill the seed feeders, then stand back and wait.

Within two minutes the first customers arrive (swarming rosy finches and bold chickadees, predictably), filling the air with merry remark. The congregation swells quickly.

As I watch the graceful play of birds, I offer a silent prayer of thanksgiving for these beautiful coinhabitants of the earth. I do not mention such thoughts to H, a nonbeliever (nevertheless he has agreed to attend Christmas Eve Mass later in the week to hear me sing). As we turn our skis back downhill, though, it strikes me that he might sympathize with this particular dimension of faith. He'd certainly agree with Pope Francis on the need for radical changes in the way humans treat the environment. That seems enough today.

"The history of our friendship with God is always linked to particular places which take on an intensely personal meaning," Francis writes in *Laudato Sì*, affirming that "the entire material universe speaks of God's love, his boundless affection for us. Soil, water, mountains: everything is, as it were, a caress of God."

On this final Sunday in Advent it's been a privilege to visit this sacred "particular place," to extend a small caress to its creatures in honor of the coming festival. And when an even greater celebration comes, that ultimate millennial day of Christ's return, I hope that there will still be birds in this clearing and that humans might venture here to join them as all the earth "sing[s] the glory of his name; give[s] to him glorious praise" (Ps 66:2).

14

Enjoying Fruition

Filling Gift Baskets with Summer Preserves

The Advent and Christmas seasons swell with images of fruition. A virgin conceives. A messiah anticipated for eons is born. Old Testament prophesies of millennial redemption and salvation are fulfilled.

What might seem paradoxical is that all of this blooming fulfillment took place historically under extremely inauspicious social conditions. At the time of Jesus' birth Israel suffered under Roman occupation—just one of a series of subjugations that had stretched for thousands of years, including captivity in Egypt and domination by Babylonia. Political unrest among the Jews themselves troubled Palestine, with zealots on the one side advocating terrorist-style violent upheaval, and a wealthy class of influential perceived collaborators, the Sadducees, compromising with the Romans. Taxation was high and the gap between rich and poor immense. Idols and commercial transactions sullied the most sacred places of Jewish worship. Though the people of Israel yearned and looked for the Messiah's coming as they had for centuries, this era might have seemed ill suited for such a glorious event.

Those of us who live in the cooler regions of the Northern Hemisphere experience another kind of paradox in the timing of our nativity observations. This one is climatic rather than political: we celebrate the coming of the Messiah who promises eternal life at a point in the year when the natural world seems mostly dead. Plants and flowers are dormant; trees have long ago lost their leaves; the ground is frozen. Even then, we know rationally, a new creation is readying itself as wild animals conceive and seeds rest and gather strength. But such incipient animation can be hard to call to mind in a month when winter, though brand new by official calendar designation, has been unleashing frigid conditions for weeks.

In such a mood a little out-of-season fruition can go a long way towards keeping the heart comforted and resolute. And so at Christmas we bring living trees (or their replicas) into our homes; we force amaryllis and narcissus into bloom. We crave clementines and grapefruits not just for their vitamin C and seasonal goodness, but also (I suspect) because their very existence proves that the sun is still shining somewhere.

My contribution to this cause of winter cheer involves offering as gifts jams and jellies, pickles and relishes canned from the past summer's harvest. I've been an enthusiastic proponent of home canning ever since my twenties; homemade preserves are delicious, and a person can indulge her creativity by concocting combinations one cannot buy in any store. It's not much more work to make a full kettle of jars than a few, and a person can only eat so many preserves on her own. There are always many jars available to give away.

It's easy to get spoiled by such handcrafted versions of staples. By late summer friends have begun sidling up to me and asking disingenuous questions like, "Have you made the blueberry-lavender jam yet?" I now wince at the taste of electric-green commercial mint jelly, conjuring the clean aroma of the pale mint-jalapeno alternative that comes from my kitchen.

There's risk involved, admittedly, in planning home-canned offerings as a major do-ahead component of Christmas giving. On processing day the produce might be fresh, the recipes tried and true, and the jars cooperative in sounding the cheery "pop!" that means they've sealed. As all canners know, however, the flavors and textures within those jars will evolve over the months ahead, and the contents may end up too sweet, too bland, or too spicy. Off tastes are not the only risk; overripe food, inexact acidity or not enough sugar, or infinitesimal contamination could turn these beautiful offerings to poison. Now and then in the interval between August and winter I go down to the basement and inspect the contents of the shelves, fretting over apparent cloudiness, worrying that the pickles look soggy rather than crisp, obsessing about the liquid levels. There's nothing to do but wait, however. Opening something to be sure it's okay means that the something can no longer be saved for the future.

The jar's glass is chilly as I take it from the basement shelf on a December afternoon less than a week before Christmas, but the ginger-peach jam inside glows with the amber warmth of a summer evening. Suddenly it is again Labor Day weekend (or labor-of-love weekend, as I once ruefully called it to a farmer's market vendor). The counter is heaped with downy fruit ready to be scalded and peeled, baskets of cucumbers and green peppers wait their turn in the laundry room. A garden bursting with geraniums, gallardia, herbs, and tomatoes is visible through the steamy kitchen window.

It's not just on Labor Day that my kitchen is full of canning steam. Between May and October a succession of irresistible bounty appears in the farmer's market and stores. In spring there's asparagus for pickling with garlic, and the first strawberries for jam; in midsummer blackberries, raspberries, corn, cucumbers, tomatoes, and peaches appear; in autumn pears and apples. The big canning kettle boils on the stove. The Mason jars, lifter, and funnel are pressed into service. The towels lining the counter become sticky with jam drips and drizzles of picking brine despite all efforts to be neat. Every year I remember how labor intensive it is to dip tomatoes into hot water so the skin comes off easily, how heavy a fully loaded batch of quart jars can be when one must lift the wire basket from the kettle and carry it to the cooling rack.

This past August anticipatory trepidation over a particular day's effort landed me in minor trouble one Sunday. "The harvest is plenty, laborers are few," Beth and I sang in the course of the communion hymn. I'd heard those words many times before, but that day the thought of ten pounds of green beans waiting to be pickled infused that text with unprecedented immediacy. *You can say that again!* my mind chimed. I started to giggle, momentarily losing the harmony line. It took Beth's sideways glance, alarmed and curious, to pull me back to the task at hand.

As much as I enjoy canning, I must admit that *in situ*, up to my elbows in green beans or peaches, I sometimes wonder why I do it. The local stores sell perfectly fine jam, delicious salsa, serviceable pickles, and adequate flavored vinegars. Better than perfectly fine varieties are available online and in specialty grocery stores in Boise and Salt Lake City.

By a session's end, though, I'm never wondering. Few satisfactions are as unambiguous and concrete as turning from the last cleanup chore at 5 p.m. to regard a counter glowing with summer-in-a-jar: scarlet salsa, dark purple plum jam spiked with five-spice powder, carrots or green beans or garlic cloves or neat slices of cucumbers glowing like jewels in clear dill-spiked brine; big glass jars of white wine vinegar packed with macerating tarragon or blackberries. As September progresses the rich scent of clove-rich pear or apple butter stewing overnight in the Crock Pot adds another layer of sensory delight.

Beyond such immediate gratification stretch happy intentions for the future. Even as I carry the jars four or five at a time down the steps to the shelves reserved for their hibernation, I've begun to dream about the months ahead when bountiful summer will turn to winter and the food in these jars and bottles will grace so many meals.

I eat some of the goods myself, holding my breath as I open each new batch to reveal whether the promise has paid off. Almost always it has. I spread pear butter on whole-wheat toast on chilly October mornings before work, spice up a roasted chicken breast with cucumber-dill relish at a November Sunday dinner. It's a joyful thing when bestirring oneself in the proper season pays such tasty rewards.

Other jars linger until the great festivals. Lara and I set out bowls of pickled green beans and rainbow carrots for the open house; raspberry vinegar and tiny spiced siekel pears will grace the year's Christmas dinner for eight.

Most of the jars, though, wait for the Christmas baskets.

∽❦ ∽❦ ∽❦

On this December day, as drifts of blowing snow fill the windows that once framed a blooming garden, I turn to the job of divvying up. I arrange jars into pretty baskets filled with raffia or tissue paper, taking care to include particular favorites for each recipient among a mix of sweet and savory offerings. I choose half pints, pints, or quarts by number of eaters in each household. I tie bows around the baskets' handles and tuck in greeting cards

When the work is complete an inspiring blanket of bounty covers the dining room table. These are only bottles of food, true, but they weave the seasons together in an intensely reassuring way. The hopes of a summer now only a memory are embodied in these offerings. The labor of their production and the patience required to wait have yielded the long-anticipated rewards.

In a small and emblematic way this moment feels sacred—a replica of the spiritual confidence Advent demands. The ever-circling year in which "there is a season [for everything], and a time for every matter under heaven" (Eccl 3:1) has come round to harvest, even though the icy winter seems less than auspicious for such an event. The cycle of months has led us back to this glorious season when we affirm Christ's birth.

The little material fruition represented by these baskets of preserves is only temporary, of course. The dispersal has left big gaps in the basement shelves; just enough jars of jams and pickles remain to see me through the winter. Before I know it June will come again and the work of preserving—and the waiting—will begin anew.

This afternoon, though, it's time to rest and rejoice, not to fret about the future. It's time to be thankful for promises fulfilled in the proper time, against apparent odds—promises as small as a jar of jam, and promises infinitely greater.

15

Resisting Temptation

Shopping at the Last Minute

I'm waiting patiently (well, sort of patiently) for the Buick in front of me to shift from reverse and move across and beyond the space it has just vacated. The man behind the wheel is obviously ancient (the tiny stature, slumped posture, the hat), the process protracted. The driver of a big pickup truck coming from the other direction is less tolerant; he darts across the elderly driver's path, nearly clipping him, right into the space I've claimed with my flashing blinker.

"You X#@@$!!!" My voice rings aloud inside the CRV, startling me as if somebody else is responsible for the outburst. Luckily all the windows are rolled up. It's late afternoon on December 23, and wet harbinger flakes of the storm foretold by last weekend's clouds have begun to drift down. I don't need a confrontation right now.

The truth is that I'd almost welcome one. People shouldn't be allowed to act so rudely without sanction, or at least shaming. Correcting the sinner strikes me as not just a canonical act of mercy, but also a righteous protest in support of social justice for the aged.

With effort I calm myself. As I finally pass the jerk (the elderly man, shaken by the near miss, has taken even longer than he might have to get himself literally in gear), I fight down the temptation to make a rude gesture. The culprit would be sure to see if I did; he's already out of his truck and walking toward the store.

In the brief interval I've been talking sense to myself. This has been a reasonably acceptable Advent for civility. I've managed to stay relatively tolerant, relatively charitable most of the time. If I'm honest I must admit that what I feel toward the pickup driver is not an unalloyed righteous rage at someone who has sinned toward another, but a sentiment primarily fueled by the blatant lack of consideration—the insult, it seems in that moment—just shown to *me*.

This is not the kind of temptation I anticipated as I ventured out to shop at the last minute before Christmas. The lure of spending money on unnecessary, redundant things set in seductive displays—maybe another holiday tablecloth now that they'd be on sale, perhaps a fancy store-bought cake, maybe extra chocolates for Christmas dinner or another bottle of wine—those were the sort of temptations that I'd counseled myself to resist.

I knew, obviously, that the shopping center would be crowded and crazy, but the exact nature of the scene remained abstract from the refuge of the living room. Thanks to a basement full of preserves and the habit of picking up presents throughout the year, I rarely experience last-minute Christmas chaos. As always, I shopped for Christmas staples a month ago (the baskets for the preserves, wrapping paper, Scotch tape, replacement Christmas light bulbs); I strategically showed up at this very grocery store at 8 a.m. a few days ago to secure Christmas dinner provisions. Early this afternoon, though, as I inventoried recipes and supplies, I discovered necessary items missing and realized that some essential staples were running low. Thus this trip to the supermarket for lemons, milk, cat food, dishwasher detergent, and flour.

Summoning perspective, I remind myself that I run on purpose almost every day and do not need a convenient parking space. I should be glad to be healthy enough to take a little hike this afternoon (and am wearing my Fitbit, so these steps will count). Less mobile people deserve the prime spots, especially on a cold evening. Bypassing the whole fray, I choose a parking space at the end of a half-empty row in Siberia, out past the liquor store in the far reaches of the shopping center.

Even walking through the parking lot to the supermarket is dangerous. Cars dart everywhere; drivers back out aggressively to force their way into the endless stalled lines. *People are so stupid. Why in the world couldn't you think ahead and shop earlier in the week?* "Watch where you're going!" I mouth through the rolled-up windows of a car that has almost collected me, resisting the urge to beat on its glass à la Dustin Hoffman in *Easy Rider*.

Inside the store, however, a very different—in truth, an astounding—atmosphere reigns. Divorced from the anonymity of their vehicles and face-to-face, people are being mostly *nice* on this Christmas Eve-Eve. The grocery aisles are as jammed and slow-moving as the parking lot aisles outside, but almost no one is pushing around others, grabbing, or making impatient remarks. People are greeting strangers with "Merry Christmas!" They wait their turn at the seafood counter, exchanging pleasantries. A woman picks up one of the two bags of fresh cranberries she's just placed in her cart (emptying the shelf) and hands it to another when she notices the second's bereft gaze.

Such shining examples of courtesy inspire me when I'm tempted to act like a jerk. I do feel irritation when access to the lemons is blocked by several couples absorbed in conversation (and seemingly not interested in lemons per se at all—this venue seems a random choice). They're wrapped up in their pleasantries, oblivious; the little kids attached to them are running around like sugar-crazed and shrieking banshees, bumping into people. Don't these adults care if others are inconvenienced by their out-of-control children? Don't they imagine that *some* people have better things to do this afternoon than to hang around a grocery store "visiting?"

I'm about to voice a rather accusatory "Excuse me!" when I recall that the pickup-truck guy is somewhere in this store; if he were in this situation he'd surely act as I've been about to act. "Hi," I greet the people who have taken up residence, mustering a friendly tone with some effort. "Would you mind if I just squeezed in here for a minute and got a few lemons?" They part immediately and with apologies. Edging my way toward the flour, I keep the streak going. I greet strangers and they smile back. I hand a jar of olives down to a woman shorter than I am who cannot reach a high shelf. I even say "Merry Christmas!" a few times.

Thoughts, lamentably, remain harder to control than actions. Even as the self-consciously nice behavior proliferates, my mind races with judgments I have no business making. One that's particularly uncharitable arrives while I'm stalled in an aisle beside a display of premade centerpieces—stiff little numbers constructed from prosaic Scotch Pine clippings (left over from unsold Christmas trees?), sprayed with glitter and adorned with plastic reindeer and Santas. "HAPPY HOLIDAY'S!" the little stick-in signs, complete with grocer's apostrophe, proclaim. A man and woman debate which to choose (can't they see that all those centerpieces are alike, all tacky and pathetic?). Snobbish contempt and pity simultaneously crest in me as they lift one from the table. Why waste money on that uninspired and ill-punctuated object when a few simple boughs and pine cones, a candle would look so much better?

I feel the same admixture of emotions toward the man buying children's presents at this late date. His cart holds a packaged doll named for a reality television celebrity *du jour*, a large monster truck, and an assembly of water guns. None of those toys is going to last very long, and if they really represent the children's taste, in my opinion those children are in trouble.

Despite such noxious musings, I'm not one of those people who approaches others and lectures them on the contents of their shopping carts (as I was once lectured when I added a bag of potato chips to the otherwise healthy contents of mine: "You were doing so well!" the officious stranger said). I have, though, caught myself in the past making a little grimace or staring with what the sensitive might take for disapproval. I try very hard on this December 23 to avoid such behavior.

It proves impossible, however, not to gaze in sad fascination at the cart ahead of mine in the checkout line. The nascent Christmas feast it contains includes a pre-thawed turkey (the kind injected with lots of fluid), three boxes of store-brand instant stuffing, four cans of generic gravy, instant mashed potatoes, refrigerator rolls that come in a tube, and several of those store-bakery cakes that I anticipated might be tempting but turned out not to be at all. No fresh vegetables or fruits are visible amid the brimming assembly.

Luckily the woman who has filled that cart appears not to be among the sensitive. She catches my gaze and smiles back. Scanning what I'm about to purchase, she nods—and Baby-Jesus-es me. "Why don't you go ahead?" she asks. "You have so few things."

Perhaps, I imagine as I wheel my purchases around hers, she's pitying me—a woman apparently with only cat food and detergent to purchase in this great orgy of Christmas preparation.

◦◦ ◦◦ ◦◦

Walking the gauntlet back to the car, driving home in traffic whose congestion does not abate until well south of the city limits, I ponder in my heart what has just transpired. It's so easy to cultivate good will toward others when one doesn't have to actually be around those others. Out in the marketplace and surrounded by December's din, however, the project of living Advent with unshakeable mercy becomes much more difficult.

I'd give myself a C- for Christian charity this afternoon. Under just a little bit of pressure, the lessons of Angel Tree Sunday and Fr. Dat vaporized.

I remember Jesus' discourse about unacted-upon nasty impulses. "If you are angry with a brother or sister, you will be liable to judgment," he instructs listeners, suggesting that the new covenant covers inappropriate thoughts as well as the actions proscribed in the Old Testament. "Everyone who looks at a woman with lust has already committed adultery with her in his heart" (Matt 5:22, 28). The takeaway is that sinning in one's mind is as bad as actually breaking the commandments.

Vowing a renewed commitment to inner charity (and registering the event for the next reconciliation), I beg forgiveness. When that acknowledgment to God is complete, I take a deep breath and recommit to interrupting the bad old cycle of spiraling either-or self-castigation. *Okay, you were hardly perfect. But you need to pick yourself up and try again. Be patient with yourself for being human. You couldn't have been the only person in that store who honored only the letter of the Old Testament law.*

Honoring the letter of the law is something, after all; it's at least a baby step in evolution above the cretin in the truck. Actually, it's more than that. The way most of us acted seems pretty darned extraordinary, given the day's pressures. Forced to deal with one another, we mustered up patience and friendliness, even small expressions of selflessness. We kept our good humor, at least in its public expression, and cooperated. Together we tacitly agreed to create an atmosphere that was almost festive inside that store. Whatever our religious affiliations or lack of them, in essence we practiced being the people that the season calls us to be.

⟡ ⟡ ⟡

"The testing of your faith produces endurance; and let endurance have its full effect, so that you may be mature and complete," writes St. James (1:3-4). And St. Peter implies that achieving spiritual maturity is not the work of an inspired instant but comes over time as a person acquires successive virtues. "You must make every effort to support your faith with goodness," he writes, "and goodness with knowledge, and knowledge with self-control, and self-control with endurance, and endurance with godliness, and godliness with mutual affection, and mutual affection with love" (2 Pet 1:5-7).

In the solitude of the car I remember how reluctant I was to go out into the mess of December's secular swirl, how certain I was that I'd encounter behavior that confirmed human insufferableness. I lost my empathy and sinned in my heart before I even left the house.

In fact a much more encouraging lesson about human nature ultimately presented itself. True, all of us (including me) were tempted to "say 'You fool'" (Matt 5:22). Yet even though we may have done that a time or two, most of us recalled ourselves to "self-control," "endurance," even "mutual affection." We rose to the occasion within the spirit of forbearance and love that Jesus preached.

If we can remember the satisfaction such behavior brings, perhaps we'll be quicker to assume those virtues in the future. At any rate, we now know that we hold the capacity for bearing patiently with each other.

And that's something to celebrate, this Christmas Eve-Eve.

16

Standing on the Threshold

Singing at Christmas Eve Mass

> Keep awake therefore, for you do not know on what day your Lord is coming. But understand this: if the owner of the house had known in what part of the night the thief was coming, he would have stayed awake and would not have let his house be broken into. Therefore you also must be ready, for the Son of Man is coming at an unexpected hour.
> —Matthew 24:42-44

The admonition to urgent conversion is one of Advent's most constant themes. The Messiah is coming into our sphere, we are assured in the season's texts and songs, and we'd better be ready. Since we cannot know the hour of his appearance, we'd be advised to begin preparing ourselves immediately. "Seek the LORD while he may be found," Isaiah advises us (55:6). Jesus' parables of the homeowner and the thief, and the wise and foolish virgins illustrate that imperative. "But about that day and hour no one knows, neither the angels of heaven, nor the Son, but only the Father," Christ says in Matthew 24:36, recalling the ancient precedent of those caught unaware by Noah's flood.

We Christians today have even less excuse than the biblical homeowner, virgins, and Israelites to be surprised with our spiritual work incomplete as Christmas dawns. There's been absolutely no mystery about when the clock will tick down, when the last door on the Advent calendar will be opened.

Yet we temporize. "The last week before Christmas is crazy," a priest once told me. "We're swamped with requests for reconciliation. I'm glad to oblige, but I do wonder why they couldn't have come to the penance service or made an appointment earlier in the month. We're swamped with donations coming in the mail, too. Kathy's constantly going to the bank."

Even with more anticipation than such folks have managed, so much of my own spiritual work always seems inadequately fulfilled as Christmas approaches. During Advent's fourth week I imagine my own lamp sputtering, at best.

◦~ ◦~ ◦~

It's not just sacred observance that's characteristically incomplete but also Christmas preparations of the secular persuasion. This year is no exception. The elaborate food gifts I planned in early December's burst of optimistic energy (when four weeks seemed a long time) will go down in the book as good intentions rather than completed projects. The butternut squash and smoked cheese intended to fill homemade ravioli find their way into a Sunday pasta dinner. The dried fruits and saffron that should have been folded into homemade panettone never even reached the shopping cart, much less the pantry. I'll be serving a boxed, most likely dry, version instead.

Neither have late nights of knitting yielded all the hoped-for results. H's fingerless mittens are finished, as is the nurse's hat. But a few of those babies (or their mothers) will receive IOUs.

It's hard enough to remember to fill the tree's water reservoir in the evenings, what with wrapping and delivering and prep-cooking for the holiday dinner and struggling to keep the house reasonably presentable for friends delivering gifts. A huge snowstorm blows in and heaps the deck and driveway with white immediately before the semester's final plagiarism hearing at the university. The neighbor who plows is at work; serious shoveling ensues. The beautiful fresh holly sent by Ford's sister in Pennsylvania is destined to become an informal, loosely-strewn quasi-table runner rather than a pretty little wreath.

One fortunate aspect of absolute deadlines, though, is that they do simplify things. While the temptation to move faster and stay up late still infiltrates December 20, 21, 22, and 23, by December 24 the only possible sane response is to take a deep breath and admit that the season is not going to go on record as a perfect Advent.

There's no sense dwelling on failures during the particular little "end time" that Christmas Eve brings. The clock has run out, and worrying over inadequacies in the details of worldly preparations would sully the joyful anticipation appropriate to the day. Obsessing about scruples and imperfections in spiritual readiness would suggest that one has not really registered a central tenet of the coming celebration—the Savior we're honoring is sublimely merciful.

I sometimes reassure myself (though this might smack of heresy) by imagining that perhaps all of those virgin's lamps were not so perfectly trimmed after all, yet the bridegroom still embraced them. Hoping that my own flawed efforts will be enough for God and for friends, I vow to do less with more attention next year.

That's next year's concern, however. Christmas Eve forces us to move ahead to a new season, into a time of fulfillment and celebration. It calls us to accept the inevitable flow of time in which every new phase of our lives and of the church year invites us to move closer to God. It insists that we echo "Let it be done to me" as we turn from the past and its regrets to accept to the new work he offers for our hands.

My Advent routine includes a built-in, non-negotiable constant that prevents even attempting to use Christmas Eve for last-minute, just-one-more-thing imperatives. At 11 a.m. each December 24, I join Beth and Brian to polish the music we'll lead at the Vigil service that evening. We don't usually rehearse in advance for Mass (we trust each other to come prepared), but meticulous readiness seems imperative for Christmas Eve. So many people who do not ordinarily attend will be present; if the music is good, it might encourage them to come again.

We gather around the piano at my friends' place. Lewis the oh-so-interested cat must, like my cats at home, be shooed from the keyboard or he will cooperate in making "music" too. First we work through the long series of Advent songs we'll sing as a prelude. It's fun to discover that the new alto harmonies I learned this season (intending to pull at least a little of my weight with these extraordinary musicians) now come with less effort than they did on Advent's first Sunday. It's good to have another chance to revisit these sweet old songs before they disappear again for a whole year.

We move on to the Christmas carols slated as hymns during the Mass. I've been practicing new harmonies for some, and this communal session provides a clear-eyed look at just how effective (or not) the effort has been. The results, as usual, are mixed. While I can hold my own against Beth's rich mezzo-soprano on several songs, others will need more attention if they're to be trotted out at any point during the next few weeks. We review the psalm and acclamation, the latter my portion this year. Though I suspect privately that the congregation would be happy to hear Beth sing both cantor components at every Mass, she offers me the priceless gift of confidence: if she sings the psalm one week, I must sing the acclamation. The following week we switch, no excuses.

When we're satisfied that we're ready, we repair to the dining room to drink coffee, eat Christmas cookies, exchange gifts, and enjoy each others' company. Eventually we decide when to meet before Mass that evening, the go about our various last-minute preparations.

Those are necessarily limited for me since the interval is too short to do much except a little house-straightening and prep-cooking. At five, as always on that day, I'm due back in town for pre-Mass Christmas cheer and a light dinner with Pamela and Russell, Elizabeth and her brother, and a few others. H also attends the gathering this year; he and these dear ones get along very well.

This intimate and decades-old festival evokes the past as well as celebrating the present. Sitting on the familiar upholstered sofa, regarding the tree decked richly with well-known ornaments, I remember when Ford and I, Russell and Pamela were four young adults with the world before us. I recall when the beautiful and confident young woman beside me was a toddler sitting on my lap, beaming up through wild blonde curls. I bring to mind Ford's last Christmas Eve, when he sat, weak but smiling and holding my hand, on this same sofa. I always feel him on this night of the year, in this place.

Given cantor responsibilities I limit the "cheer" to one glass of wine but nevertheless feel very merry. As our laughter rings, I remember the account of a long-ago holiday gathering depicted in that great poem about grief and healing, Alfred, Lord Tennyson's "In Memoriam A. H. H." One member is also missing from the party depicted there, yet as with this one, the participants

> . . . keep the day. With festal cheer,
> With books and music, surely we
> Will drink to him, whate'er he be,
> And sing the songs he loved to hear.

It feels good to take time for this familiar family pleasure as the light fades on this sacred night, to stop thinking about all the must-dos and concentrate on the opportunity to enjoy loved ones old and new.

I leave forty-five minutes before the others for last-minute practice. Even though it's early, we three musicians are not the only people in the church. Some of the early birds are eager-beaver parishioners who fear that they won't get good seats if their cars are not among the first in the parking lot. Others are the elderly, who prefer to take their places while the aisles are still uncrowded. A handful of people kneel, deep in prayer. All of these hear our last practice, complete with joshing and do-overs and moments that sound better than the actual Mass singing will because we're more relaxed. We're three people who love making music together for God and everybody and ourselves, and I hope that our joy is contagious.

"Time?" Beth asks and Brian checks his watch. Practice transitions to prelude. We begin with "O Come, O Come, Emanuel," reaching back to the old-testament longing, then sing "The

Angel Gabriel," referencing the very start of the Advent story, then move along in rough chronology: "See How the Virgin Waits For Him," "People Look East," "The King Shall Come When Morning Dawns," revisiting the songs we love the best. As each finishes I find myself saying farewell; when Beth glances at me I sense that she feels the same.

Immersed fleetingly again in the spirit of Advent, I imagine scenes that will not return for a year: the wreath party, the evening I wrote the Christmas letter, the hours spent cooking for the big party with Lara, the snowy clearing where we filled bird feeders. Such little things, all those ordinary Advent activities. Such sacred things.

More and more people arrive, and by the time the prelude ends the church is so packed that we cannot see the back vestibule where the priest and altar servers wait. I do, though, glimpse my friends in the next-to-last pew; they've come just in time to claim seats.

It's 8:05 p.m.; Mass should be beginning. Beth climbs to the high step behind us where additional choir members would stand if there were any and peers over the throng of humanity so that we do not miss Fr. John's signal.

Oh so soon, it seems, she is back beside me announcing the opening hymn, and Brian's hands are sounding the introduction. Even as a final jolt of bittersweet nostalgia sweeps me (*Advent is over, definitively, for another year*), I find my initial alto note among his chords and hold it determinedly inside my head.

Right on cue our voices sound together, inviting everyone in that church into one song of celebration, one invitation to open to God's grace. Other voices swell to join us, proclaiming the new season, leaning into whatever calls and struggles, whatever joys and deepening of faith it might bring. "O come, all ye faithful," the words soar, and suddenly it is Christmas.

Acknowledgments

Scripture texts in this work are taken from the *New Revised Standard Version Bible: Catholic Edition* © 1989, 1993, Division of Christian Education of the National Council of the Churches of Christ in the United States of America. Used by permission. All rights reserved.

Excerpts from the English translation of the *Catechism of the Catholic Church* for use in the United States of America copyright © 1994, United States Catholic Conference, Inc.—Libreria Editrice Vaticana. English translation of the *Catechism of the Catholic Church: Modifications from the Editio Typica* copyright © 1997, United States Catholic Conference, Inc.—Libreria Editrice Vaticana. Used with Permission.

Introduction
Michael J. Taylor, introduction to *The Sacraments: Readings in Contemporary Sacramental Theology*, ed. Michael J. Taylor (Staten Island, NY: Alba House, 1981). © Society of St. Paul.

Chapter 1
Liturgical Music Today © 1982, United States Catholic Conference (USCC), Washington, DC 20017-1194. Used by permission.

Chapter 2
Thomas Merton, *Seeds of Contemptlation* (New York: New Directions, 1949). © 1949, Our Lady of Gethsemani Monastery.

Chapter 6
Tad W. Guzie, "Why They Changed Communion," *U.S. Catholic* 41, no. 9 (1976): 100–105.

Chapter 11

Dietrich Bonhoeffer, *God is in the Manger: Reflections on Advent & Christmas*, trans. O. C. Dean Jr., ed. Jana Riess (Louisville, KY: Westminster John Knox, 2010).

Chapter 13

"Philosophy of Land Use," Monastery of St. Gertrude, 465 Keuterville Road, Cottonwood, Idaho 83522 © June 9, 1993; https://www.stgertrudes .org/about/careoftheland/. Used by permission.

"Of All Good Gifts," Conference of American Benedictine Prioresses © 1980. Used by permission.